The enemy w

Radical feminism in the Christian churches

Edited by Christine M Kelly

Foreword by Prof Alice von Hildebrand

THE ENEMY WITHIN
Radical feminism in the Christian churches

ISBN 1 871217 10 5

by the same editor and publisher
Feminism v. Mankind

published by
FAMILY PUBLICATIONS
Wicken, Milton Keynes, MK19 6BU, U K
Telephone: **0908 57234** *Fax:* **0908 57331**

cover design by
Joanna Pitt

typeset in Plantin by
Avocet Typesetters, Bicester, Oxon

printed in England by
BPCC Wheatons Ltd
Marsh Barton, Exeter, EX2 8RP

Contents

Contents

Foreword

G K Chesterton defines a feminist as "one who dislikes the chief feminine characteristics". (*What is wrong with the World*, p 197.) He is right: feminism wages war on femininity, and unwittingly labours toward a total victory of men over women. Being a knight for femininity, Chesterton used the spear of his witticism to oppose feminism: "I want to destroy the tyranny. They (the feminists) want to destroy the womanhood". (*What is wrong with the World*, p 199.)

Feminism is self-defeating: it basically aims at aping male characteristics, and inevitably leads to radical sterility: whether religious, moral, artistic, human or sexual. It is prompted by a spirit of bitterness and resentment and tramples down upon the "mystery of femininity" characterized by sacredness, receptivity, openness to the divine.

It is worth remarking that feminism originated in Scandinavian and Anglo-Saxon countries where the cult of Mary – Theotokos – is either non-existent or has been watered down by the prevalent culture. The countries where the devotion to the one blessed among women is strong and alive (whether Latin countries or Eastern Christendom) have been preserved from this scourge. It is not by accident that feminism wages its most vicious attacks on both purity and maternity, for Mary is both Virgin and Mother. Devotion to Mary – who has crushed the serpent's head – is clearly the best antidote against feminism.

"I do not deny that women have been wronged and even tortured . . ." (Chesterton, *What is wrong with the World*, p 148). This fact, which cries to heaven, has led many people to assume that feminism is a movement exclusively motivated by the laudable desire to right these wrongs. Alas, how many women are battered, abused and murdered; how many are raped, even at a very young age. No word is strong enough to condemn these abominations.

No doubt the feminists have played this card, but anyone who cares to study the philosophy behind these recriminations, will soon discover that it is animated by a spirit of metaphysical rebellion unrelated to the above mentioned crimes.

The present volume contains a broad spectrum of essays which aim at diagnosing the virus contained in feminist philosophies. It is a must for anyone who wishes to get acquainted with the goals of the feminist agenda.

One essay brilliantly highlights the pagan roots of feminism, which actually leads to self-worship; others illustrate the same point by describing the horrors of feminist liturgies, and the secular humanism that animates their philosophy; others again document how radical feminists have insidiously infiltrated social work, education, parishes, religious organizations; others reveal how radical feminism, and the ordination of women, have brought havoc in Anglican communities; another discloses the sway that leading feminists have in Australia. One essay is dedicated to the Orthodox approach to femininity, viewed as an image of Mary, the Theotokos; another again unveils the heresy of feminism. Finally we are offered a magnificent essay on the beauty, nature and greatness of femininity.

These essays are so rich in insights that it is not possible to do them justice in a brief introduction. They deserve a careful perusal, and admirably complement each other. They are all centred on the seriousness of the threat that feminist philosophies pose for Christianity. All of them agree that the ordination of women runs counter to their nature, their mission, their charism. Christ – our Saviour and King – has chosen men (not women) to be his apostles and his priests; He in whom we find "all the treasures of wisdom and science", has decided that the priesthood should be reserved

to men. Women therefore cannot be ordained. But Christ
too decided to have a human mother and no human father;
consequently, women are called upon to be the mothers of
priests, and it was Mary who became the mother of the Priest
par excellence: Christ, the Saviour of the world. The
Godman, who had a perfect knowledge of human nature,
while giving to a woman – his mother – the choicest role
in the economy of redemption, has granted some privileged
males a mission adapted to man's "icon", to his particular
charism: the priesthood. The latter was neither a decision
dictated (as weak-headed sociologists would have us believe)
by the climate of the time, nor handed down by a tradition
rooted in patriarchalism. No, it is to be traced back to a sacred
tradition based on the all-wise decision of him who alone
knows perfectly the secrets of man's nature, and the
particular calling best adapted to this nature.

Whether because the feminists have managed to conquer
the newsmedia, or because they espouse ultra-liberal causes
which are the fashion of the day, or again because of
cowardice, one cannot deny that there are many in positions
of authority who let themselves be cowered by feminist
outbursts and intimidated by their rhetoric.

All virtues are required of Christians, but there is one virtue
which is of crucial importance for those in positions of
authority: namely *Moral Courage*. Indeed, one needs courage
to swim against the tide, and to oppose the spirit of the time
which is very rarely in harmony with the promptings of the
Holy Spirit.

One needs moral courage to take the defence of femininity
against feminism. Indeed, according to God's redemptive
plan, women who have not been given the keys of the
Kingdom, nevertheless have been given a key position which,
when rightly used, will enable them – following Mary's
example – to "crush the serpent's head". But when this
same key is used in a spirit of revolt and rebellion, it can
actually lead to the destruction of marriage, of the family,

7

of society at large, and shake the Church down to its very foundation.

May our religious leaders courageously lead the fight against the evil of feminism, which Cardinal Ratzinger rightly assesses to be at the very root of the immoralism so prevalent today. May the Holy Virgin, the sweet flower of Jesse, who is simultaneously as strong as an army arrayed in battle, intercede for our leaders that they may have the supernatural strength to fight the spirit of the time. May they overcome the false humility which besets some of them, tempted, as they are, to confuse their person and their office. For this reason they often shirk from using their God-given authority being plagued by a bad conscience and painfully aware of their own inadequacies. May they realize that feminism is the greatest enemy of femininity, and that he alone who has a tender devotion to Mary – Virgin and Mother – can understand the unique role assigned to the female sex in the economy of redemption.

Alice von Hildebrand
New York, March 1992

About the Authors

Dori Watson Boynton is a housewife and lives in Florida. Grounded in scripture and church history with five years in a religious order, she is a retired professional teacher and lecturer. She is a counsellor, retreat conductor, editor and writer. She has a Masters degree in the History of Art, specializing in stylistic analysis and form criticism and has had several books published in this field. She is currently undertaking the formation of The Guild of Anglican Women, an association for women of the Traditional Anglican Communion. Her husband is a bishop of the traditional Anglican Catholic Church. She paints icons when time allows.

Yves Dubois was born in Brussels in 1938. He read Theology at London University and trained for the Orthodox priesthood at Saint Vladimir Seminary, New York. He was ordained priest in Montreal in 1966. He has taught French and R.S. at Ealing Abbey (1969-1980) and at Downside Abbey since 1980; was on the staff of Russian parishes in London (1967-1980) and founded the English Language Community of St John of Kronstadt in Bath in 1980. He is much concerned with restoring sound Biblical teaching and community life to parishes. He is married with two sons.

Babette Francis was born in India but has lived in Australia since 1953. She has a BSc in microbiology and has worked in the pharmaceutical industry and as a journalist and editor. She is a founder member of Women Who Want to be Women and is its national and overseas co-ordinator. She has contributed articles to a wide variety of publications worldwide, including the anthology *Feminism v. Mankind*.

9

Cornelia Ferreira is a writer and lecturer who lives in Toronto, Canada and is a full-time mother of four children. She has a BSc in Chemistry from Marianopolis College and an MSc from Sir George William (Concordia) University, both in Montreal. She is the head of Women for Faith and Family, Canada, and edits its newsletter. Her other publications include *The Feminist Agenda within the Catholic Church*, *The Emerging Feminist Religion*, *Feminism v. Mankind*, RENEW: *A tree rooted in Modernism and the New Age Movement*, and *The New Age Movement – the Kingdom of Satan on Earth*. Her articles have been published in *Homiletic and Pastoral Review*, *Challenge* and elsewhere.

Alice von Hildebrand is a Professor Emeritus (the first female Professor of Philosophy) at Hunter College, City University, New York, and an internationally known author and lecturer. In recent years she has specialized in matters pertaining to women. Her latest book *By Love Refined, Letters to a Young Bride* addresses itself to the newly-married and has won critical acclaim in the United States and Europe. She was married to philosopher Dietrich von Hildebrand, "a twentieth century doctor of the Church".

Christine M Kelly has a Masters Degree in the History of Art and Design. She is a Deputy Director of Family & Youth Concern, school governor in both the state and independent sectors and has written and presented educational material for schools. She edited the anthology *Feminism v. Mankind*. She is married with four children.

William Oddie is a former Fellow of St Cross College, Oxford. He is a writer and regular commentator on church affairs on TV and in the press and is the author of *What will happen to God?* and *The Crockford File, 1988*. He is currently working on a new biography of G K Chesterton. Formerly an Anglican clergyman, he and his family were received into the Catholic Church in 1991.

Valerie Riches is married with two children and trained as a social worker. As Director of the Family Education Trust and Family & Youth Concern she has contributed widely in the national press and on radio and television. She has lectured in all five continents and is the author of several publications including *Sex & Social Engineering*, *Who Cares for Children?* , and *Feminism v. Mankind.* She founded the Association of Catholic Women in 1988, of which she is Vice-Chairman, and was elected a Catholic Woman of the Year in 1992.

Josephine Robinson was educated at St Anthony's, Sherborne and St Hilda's College, Oxford, where she was an Exhibitioner and read English. She has worked for Christian Aid and as Chairman of the Family Welfare Committee of the Order of Christian Unity. She is Chairman of the Association of Catholic Women and a pro-life counsellor and speaker. In 1991 she was elected as one of the Catholic Women of the Year. She is married with three grown-up children.

John Saward was born in Middlesex in 1947, and is married with three daughters. He was educated at Hampton Grammar School and St John's College, Oxford. Before being received into the Catholic Church in 1979, he was Junior Research Fellow and (Anglican) Chaplain of Lincoln College, Oxford. Since 1980 he has been Professor of Dogmatic Theology at Ushaw College, Durham. In the summer of 1992 he takes up a similar post at St Charles Borromeo Seminary, Philadelphia. His publications include *Perfect Fools, The Mysteries of March,* and *Christ, the Light of the Nations.* He is one of the translators of the works of Hans Urs von Balthasar.

11

ABOUT THE AUTHORS

Pat Taylor is a professional actress and musician and lives in Sydney, Australia. An Anglican, she is Director of Challenge Ministries, an inter-denominational organization distributing Bible Study seminars on Marriage and Family. She is married with five children.

One

The Bishops' Dilemma

Radical Feminism within the Catholic Church of England and Wales

Christine Kelly and Valerie Riches

The original meaning of "feminism" was a belief in theory and practice of equal rights for women. Feminism as a political force came into being in the nineteenth century as the suffragette movement, whose original goals for civic reform and the legitimate right to vote paved the way for equal pay for equal work, vocational opportunity and openness within the professions. These feminists were, by and large, high-minded family women who were concerned to eradicate injustices against women, not with female supremacy.

However, over the last thirty years pressure for radical feminist policies has become pervasive and determined. As a result, the legitimate right for the removal of discrimination against women has been overtaken and superseded by feminist political extremism seeking power in all fields of human activity, including the Christian churches.

The demands of secular feminists and religious feminists have become inseparable. In the Roman Catholic Church the call for the ordination of women and a female-centred theology may predominate the arguments, but the ordination issue is merely the tip of the iceberg. They also want the Church to change its traditional teachings on divorce and remarriage, and on artificial contraception and abortion as women's rights. The more radical among them seek lesbian

13

and 'gay' liberation and see the role of husbands and fathers as expendable. In line with secular feminists they regard child rearing as oppressive and seek the provision of full-time childcare facilities.

Throughout history those who sought to destroy the Church knew that this could best be achieved from within its structures. Radical feminists too, realised that this strategy would be the most effective. Significant numbers now hold key positions in the Church in administration, teaching and feminist studies. In 1985, after a 'Women and Spirituality' conference Rosemary Radford Ruether, the American feminist theologian, advised Catholic feminists to give the appearance of legitimate 'Catholicity' in its power bases " . . . as camouflage while revolutionising from within".

How can the Catholic bishops, collegially and in all good faith, deal with this subversion in the Church? There are, of course, very good pastoral reasons for listening to the myriad of views expressed, but what weight should be given to them, and how representative are they of the general view? Are they listened to and apparently attended to more often because they come from articulate, well-organised pressure groups?

The bishops are in the difficult and unenviable position of seeking to hold the Church together in all her diversity, with charity and wisdom. They must be mindful of the needs of all the faithful. Yet the time has now surely come when they can no longer encompass the clamour and power-seeking of radical feminism within the Church and still protect unsuspecting Catholic women. The evidence contained in the following pages indicates that such a compromise is no longer possible and that there is a need for strong ecclesiastical leadership.

The Emerging Feminist Network

In 1968 the Papal Encyclical *Humanae Vitae*, proscribing artificial contraception, was promulgated. For those who had been operating a network of dissent within the Catholic

Church the encyclical provided a new focus. In partnership with feminists the network promoted and exploited opposition to the Church's teaching authority. From now on dissent in the Roman Catholic Church became integral to the emerging feminist network.

In 1970 the Women's Liberation Movement[1] held its first conference at Oxford in which it laid down the movement's demands for equal pay, educational and job opportunities, free contraception, abortion on demand and 24-hour nurseries for all children under five. At the same time a radical ecumenical organisation, One for Christian Renewal (known as One) was set up in the churches with its Catholic input coming from the politicized 1960s network. Lumen Books was also set up to import and distribute feminist literature from North America into the churches.

At about the same time, in 1972, the first radical seeds were sown in the Anglican Church when the militant Christian Parity Group was set up and aligned itself with the Women's Liberation Movement. Its founder, Una Kroll, wants "political ordination for women".[2] Significantly, she claims to have helped to set up two organisation in 1978, the Anglican's Movement for the Ordination of Women (MOW) and the Oxford-based Christian Women's Information and Resource Centre (CWIREC);[3] the former bringing the Christian unity movement to a virtual halt and the latter, based on the Dominican House at Oxford, acting as a resource centre for the overall Christian feminist movement in the churches. Throughout the 1970s the women's movement was increasingly seen by the far left as one of the most effective methods for radicalisation, as the Communist Party was rightly to observe in 1990:

> The women's movement has taught us the subversive power of non-violence.[4]

In society and in the Catholic Church, the wide acceptance of the contraceptive pill, allegedly liberating women, was followed by an equally steep increase in the divorce rate. It was on the back of this moral rebellion in the Church that feminism and its call for women priests was able to establish itself. As a leader of the Catholic Women's Network, Alexina Murphy, was to say:

> As Catholics we may gain some insight into why the Magisterium is against contraception and against the ordination of women, two apparently disparate issues which are none the less fundamentally allied.[5]

The 1980 Feminist Network

In 1977 the organisation Roman Catholic Feminists was set up and amongst them was the Dorcas Group whose leader, Dora Turbin,[6] had worked closely with the anti-*Humanae Vitae* Catholic Renewal Movement. According to a radical feminist resource book, she has the avowed aim " . . . of eliminating the clergy altogether".[7]

By the mid 1980s another feminist organisation St Joan's International Alliance (SJIA) was being run from a secretariat at 36 Court Lane, Dulwich in South London. This small, militant, single issue organisation is now committed to the fight for women priests within the Catholic Church. According to its secretary, Ianthe Pratt:

> We need to develop, or return to, election by the community rather than self-selection of the leader of the community, by bishops and clergy.[8]

In 1984 members of the SJIA set up the high profile Catholic Women's Network (CWN) and gradually the pieces of the 1980s radical feminist network in the Catholic Church were being put together.

The CWN's inaugural meeting at St. Mary's Catholic Teacher Training College,[9] was addressed by a feminist theologian, Rosemary Radford Ruether, who had recorded in her autobiography that (her devotion) . . . to Mary was somewhat less than her devotion to some far more powerful divine females that she knew: Isis, Athena and Artemis.[10]

In 1989, according to Alexina Murphy of the CWN,

we recognise that changes which last in the Church are ones which become built into the structures. That's what we want to do, to change the structures.[11]

What seemed to be a string of spontaneously formed organisations nationwide, was however, in reality, a network being run from a semi-detached house in Dulwich, by a secretariat which had been active in this kind of networking for two decades. The same names cropped up frequently in several of these Dulwich organisations. Anyone unaware of this tangled network could be forgiven for believing that a sizable groundswell of radical feminist opinion existed throughout the Church. In fact such views were represented by a few highly active and so-called "loyal dissenters". (see Appendix A)

Consolidating the Network

In 1985 the Secretariat of the Bishops' Conference published a list of organisations on which the Bishops based their submissions to Rome for the Extraordinary Synod of that year. Incredibly, three out of the four that were listed "national" organisations were[12] dedicated to promoting women priests and feminism and even more incredibly were based at the same address in Dulwich. Speaking on behalf of the Bishops' Conference its secretary, Mgr Vincent Nichols said that they regretted

. . . the failure to come to terms with the role of women in the Church, (that) attention must be paid to exclusive language (and that) there must be an effort by the whole Church to be open to the changing role of women.[13]

It was as if a radical feminist from the network had written it for him.

1986 saw the first UK conference calling for women priests in the Catholic Church. It was organised from Dulwich by SJIA, with its speaker Kathy Walsh, a Westminster Diocesan Education Officer, saying:

We may have to join the club to change the rules.[14]

1986 also saw the CWN's report to the Bishops on the forthcoming Synod on the Laity, called *Listen Bishop*. It was drafted with the help of Jenny Bond, a founder member of the CWN and assistant to the Secretary of the Bishops' Conference of England and Wales, Mgr Vincent Nichols.

In 1987 another part of the 1980s network was set up consisting of a bi-annual meeting of feminists at Heythrop College, known simply as the Women's Ad Hoc Group.[15] Out of their first meeting came the decision to try to get a women's committee set up inside the Bishops' Conference and also to establish an Association for Inclusive Language (AIL). This second decision was implemented and a new network organisation sprang up, once again run from Dulwich.

Thus by 1987 the main structures of the feminist network within the Church were the Catholic Women's Network (CWN), the Women's Ad Hoc Group, the St Joan's International Alliance (SJIA), Lumen Books, the Association for Inclusive Language (AIL), and the Christian Women's Resource Centre (CWRC) which had been set up in 1981. All the last four organisations are based at Dulwich and appropriately the CWRC also calls itself The Dulwich Centre. At the 1987 Women's Ad Hoc Group meeting at Heythrop, four women were delegated the task of approaching the Bishops' Conference, but the idea of a women's committee being attached to the Conference was rejected. However, by way of compromise and without the formal requirements asked of other organisations, the SJIA and its sibling organisation the CWN were admitted to the National Board of Catholic Women (NBCW). The NBCW is the main

18

women's consultative body to the Bishop's Conference, representing over thirty women's organisations. So now the feminist movement within the Church had two bases, one at Dulwich and also a foothold in the NBCW. Within a year the penetration of radical feminist influences in the NBCW were such that the CWN membership secretary, Anne Leeming, was appointed to the important position of secretary of the NBCW.

Power and Manipulation

By 1989 a small number of activists had achieved a high degree of infiltration into the Church. Frequently, as if to "empower" the network, alternative liturgies were introduced at network meetings. "Power" is a word which appears repeatedly in these liturgies and replaces the humility of asking for grace. The militant agenda of secular feminism is thus transferred to a religious context with power being demanded of a hermaphrodite God, to be used according to the will of feminists. A typical example took place during Holy Week in 1989 which had been organised by a Catholic organisation called Catholic People's Weeks (CPW).[16] The Easter Sunday Mass took the form of using,

> . . . symbols and silences to pull the group away from relying on their verbal skills. This bears fruit in liturgies involving mime, dance and actions which conclude the Mass with the entire group bound, giggling hysterically, in a skein of woollen threads and then in a round of enthusiastic hymn singing which ends in spontaneous dancing and jiving to music of the group's guitars.[17]

Indeed, not only is it felt necessary to create alternative liturgies but to conduct them outside church buildings. As Sue Walker of the Catholic People's Weeks said:

> No amount of liturgical reform is going to correct a basic unsoundness in the way of our sacramental ministry

whereby we "wall off" the "godless" world and enter into the holy Temple.[18]

Lesbianism, in the form of the Catholic Lesbian Sisterhood, became featured boldly in CWN literature.[19] At Network meetings, such is the dislike of the hierarchical and patriarchal Church that Holy Mass is rarely said, but rather alternative liturgies. To fill the void, new ones are constantly being constructed. These included an evening in April 1990 when Mary Hunt, the lesbian theologian, explained that in her view,

> . . . a revolution (is) taking place outside of orthodox church structures, outside of the organised institution, involving people who want to be church but find the organised set up is not enough, does not offer enough to contain their experience as women.[20]

Apparently, according to Mary Hunt there are

> . . . literally hundreds, perhaps thousands of nuns in the US who don't go near church any more.[21]

Alternative liturgies are a particular speciality of the women's movement, having strong pagan overtones. They cultivate symbolic activities, such as "apple blessing" and "green ribbon liturgy" used at joint CWN and Catholic Lesbian Sisterhood sexual orientation workshops, with its symbolic "bonding". As a CWN newsletter put it:

> Other groups have formed worshipping communities which can experiment with non-sexist liturgies and create an environment in which women do not feel distanced and alienated . . . in the Catholic Church we have the SJIA and the CWN.[22]

Sr Myra Poole, Contact Secretary for the CWN, and the St Joan's International Alliance representative on the NBCW, reported on a Women in Ministry day at the Jesuit's Heythrop College, saying:

> All participants were anointed with symbolic oil and

Suzanne Fageol (an American priestess) led us in a Circle Dance.[23]

The Catholic Women's Network (CWN) holds conscious-ness-raising sessions designed to indoctrinate women into the feminist mindset. Increasingly, by various techniques of consciousness-raising, the call for women priests has been heard in the Catholic Church. In 1990 the process took a step forward with a so-called "consultation" of women by the National Board of Catholic Women. In parishes throughout the country women were asked to reply to a NBCW consultation paper used to stimulate discussion and written by a leading member of the SJIA, Kathy Walsh. The paper assumed dissent and contained such questions as:

> Can you give examples from your own experience of discrimination and marginalisation in the Church . . . ? Did Jesus ordain priests in the way we have come to understand the practice?[24]

Keen to get information, the organisers asked the groups replying to send in personal information, adding that it was,

> . . . essential that all differing viewpoints and experiences are recorded.[25]

It was the ideal way for developing the network into a nation-wide movement within the Church, with allegedly the Roman Catholic hierarchy having been supportive of the consultation document. Yet it is clear that a self-selected group of respondents, replying to questions so framed as to elicit a certain response and analysed partially, cannot be considered valid. When the resulting report called *Do Not Be Afraid* was published, Cardinal Hume said he was sympathetic but did not believe the views expressed in the report were the general view.[26]

Yet as if to reinforce the assumptions made in the consultation documents, Angela Perkins, spokeswoman for the NBCW, claimed that

21

many women feel very frustrated and hurt by Church structures, we need the active support of the Bishops themselves to change these structures so as to include women in the decision-making process of Church life.[27]

In her report to the SJIA about the NBCW, Kathy Walsh said:

. . . there was a less subservient atmosphere now evident on the Board, who no longer waited to hear the views of the bishops before acting.[28]

It had taken almost a decade to set up the overall feminist network within the Catholic Church, with each of its organisations serving a different purpose. At the heart of it all is a small core of activists and a group of organisations run from the same address in Dulwich. (See Appendix B)

By 1990 the SJIA and the CWN had become official Catholic organisations listed as such under the heading "with ecclesiastical approval" in the *National Catholic Directory*. The CWN membership secretary had taken over as secretary of the National Board of Catholic Women (NBCW). Lumen Books was feeding radical feminist literature from North America into the churches from its Dulwich base. In diocese after diocese the NBCW's so-called "consultation of women" was heading the consciousness-raising of the Church, run by a handful of activists from the SJIA-CWN network.

By March 1991 the co-ordinators of the militant SJIA and the CWN, Ianthe Pratt and Alexina Murphy, had been co-opted onto NBCW sub-committees that had just been set up. But as if to cap it all, in April 1992 Pat Jones, a member of the CWN, was appointed as the first woman assistant general secretary to the English and Welsh Bishops' Conference.

Radical Feminist Plans beyond the 1990s

The successful infiltration of so many Church structures is, however, only the first step. The Network now seeks to

22

inculcate its ideology at the deepest levels in the Church, forcing change to take place. In order to do this it needs, above all, "Episcopal credibility" and "Episcopal mandate".

A 1991 survey of the North American feminist movement in the Church called *Ungodly Rage*,[29] described a change of policy which took place in the mid-1980s in the Canadian Church and which is now being repeated in the Catholic Church in England and Wales. Instead of approaching individual bishops, it was decided to work through the Conferences of Bishops in individual countries. The mistake that the American feminists had made was to target several bishops whom they converted to such an extent that their fellow-Bishops were wary of them. Thus, the movement ended up with just these bishops.

Consequently the Canadian feminists, rather than working through individual bishops, worked with devastating effect through the Canadian Conference, setting up a dialogue which proved successful in this larger forum.

Similarly, in England and Wales, "Episcopal credibility" is being achieved. Network organisations are listed in the National Catholic Directory and an "Episcopal mandate" given to hold an on-going national consultation of women in diocese after diocese.

Yet, despite being given their own dialogue committee with the Bishop's Conference, they are still faced with a major problem. How do they get their message, with all their "credibility", to permeate the parishes and pews of the Church?

In order to expand their influence and lines of communication in the Church, active feminists appear to be trying to push for change in at least five identifiable areas:

1. To set up, with Episcopal approval, **Diocesan Committees** for women's issues.

2. To set up, with Episcopal approval, **Diocesan Contact Persons** to "liaise" with the Bishop on women's issues.

3. To get a separate **Women's Page** (or column) in Diocesan newspapers or magazines.

4. To appoint **Parish Contact Persons** to "assist" the episcopally approved, on-going process of the National Consultation of Women.

5. At parish and deanery level, to locate and identify alienated and dissenting **Deacon's Wives.**

Each Bishop will recognise the kinds of initiatives mentioned above. He may well, believing them to be worthy, have sanctioned their establishment and encouraged them to flourish – the real agenda being unsuspected by him. The aim is not to strengthen the Church but to force it to change, not by general consent in an evolutionary way, but by stealth and revolution.

What the Pope teaches

As early as 1983, well aware of the threat to the Church posed by radical feminism, Pope John Paul II told a group of American Bishops:

> The Bishops must give proof of their pastoral ability and leadership by withdrawing all support from individuals and groups who in the name of progress, justice or compassion, or for any other alleged reason, promote the ordination of women to the priesthood.[30]

He added:

> In so doing, such individuals or groups are in effect damaging the very dignity of women that they profess to promote and advance.[31]

Anyone these days, who speaks out against the excesses of feminism, is liable to be pilloried and none more so than a celibate clergy. Nevertheless serious damage and individual suffering to men and women will follow unless the words of the Pope are heeded. He also said:

All efforts made against the truth are destined to produce not only failure but acute personal frustration.[32]

As if to confirm the rightness of this assessment a poem by Marisa Lincoln entitled *Ode to Mother Church* which is full of bitterness and hatred for the Catholic Church, appeared in the Catholic Women's Network journal. The penultimate verse of this long and vituperative ode reads:

You (The Church) die now inside your ancient bolted deathbound gates for your festering lies clutching your keys to a Loveless Kingdom . . .[33]

Back in 1983 the Holy Father foresaw what lay ahead and might have been addressing all Bishops facing the dilemma of radical feminism when he said:

Whatever the Bishops can do to prevent this failure and frustration by explaining the truth, is an act not only of pastoral charity but of prophetic leadership.[34]

Radical feminism within the Catholic Church in England and Wales has brought the Church to the point where that prophetic leadership is desperately needed.

REFERENCES

1. The two main organisations of the international Women's Liberation Movement are, the Womens International Information and Communication Service (ISIS) and the International Feminist Network.
2. Una Kroll, "The Christian Parity Group", ed. Rex Ambler and David Haslam, *Agenda for Prophets*, 1980, pp 26-27.
3. CWIREC based at the Dominican House of Studies, Oxford, serves the Christian Feminist Movement.
4. *Marxism today*, Communist Party Membership Advertisement, April 1990.
5. Alexina Murphy, "TV Spotlight on the Hidden Agenda of Women's Roles", *Catholic Herald*, 10 September, 1989.
6. Dora Turbin, leader of the Dorcas Group and a member of the Christian Renewal Movement, SJIA and the CWN.
7. *Feminist Action One*, p 90.
8. Ianthe Pratt, *The Catholic Citizen*, Summer, 1985.
9. St Mary's Teacher Training College, Strawberry Hill.
10. R. Radford Ruether, *Journeys: The Impact of Personal Experience on Religious Thoughts*, Paulist, New York, 1975.

11. Alexina Murphy, "Hoping for Women Priests", *Movement for the Ordination of Women,* 1989, p 12.
12. *The Universe,* 2 August, 1985.
13. Msgr. Vincent Nichols, Secretary to the Bishops' Conference of England and Wales, *The Universe,* 2 August 1985.
14. Kathy Walsh, "Women Priests? Why Not?", *The Universe,* 4 August 1986.
15. This bi-annual meeting of the network agreed not to give itself a name.
16. Catholic People's Weeks (CPW) was first listed in the national Catholic Directory in 1959. It provides inexpensive holidays with a theological flavour. In recent times various 'weeks' have been markedly radical and feminist. CPW's present chairman is Anne Worden, wife of Peter Worden founder and chairman of the Catholic Renewal Movement (CRM).
17. Paul Vallely, "Easter Week Diary", *The Tablet,* March 1989.
18. *Network,* Journal of the Catholic Women's Network, Spring 1991.
19. CWN featured CLS from the time it was set up, co-sponsoring events with it.
20. Joanna Moorhead, *Catholic Herald,* 18 May 1990.
21. Catholic Women's Network, *Newsletter,* March 1990.
22. *Ibid.,* December 1989.
23. *Ibid.,* March 1987.
24. Kathy Walsh and Angela Perkins, "Status and Role . . . Life and Mission", Discussion Paper 1, NBCW, 1989.
25. *Ibid.*
26. "Cardinal rejects Simple Solution to win Popularity, *The Independent,* 7 May 1991.
27. "A Call to Women", *New Day Magazine,* May 1990.
28. Kathy Walsh, St Joan's International Alliance, AGM, 10 March 1990.
29. D. Steichen, *Ungodly Rage,* San Francisco, Ignatius Press, 1991.
30. Pope John Paul II, address to 23 American Bishops, Castel Gandolfo, 5 September 1983.
31. *Ibid.*
32. *Ibid.*
33. *Newsletter,* Journal of the Catholic Women's Network, Spring 1991.
34. Pope John Paul II, *op. cit.*

APPENDIX A

By 1990 the network consisted of, or was associated with, the following organisations. Suffixes indicate:

A Anglican Organisation
E Ecumenical Organisation
36 Run wholly or in part from 36 Court Lane, Dulwich

1968	Pastoral Development Group (linked with IDOC)	36
1968	Catholic Renewal Movement (Feminist research interests)	36
1968	Newman Association Family Committee	36
1968	Newman Association Theological Studies Group	36
1972	Lumen Books	36
1976	Christian Parity Group	A
1976	Homosexual and Gay Christian Movement	E
1977	Movement for the Ordination of Married Men (MOMM)	
1977	Roman Catholic Feminists (Dorcas Group)	
1977	Christian Feminist Movement	E

1978	Christian Women's Information and Resource Centre	E
1978	Movement for the Ordination of Women (MOW)	A
1979	Feminist Theology Project (linked with Christian Organisations for Social, Political and Econcomic Change - COSPEC)	E
1979	Catholic Lesbian Sisterhood	
1981	Christian Women's Resource Centre	36
1981	COSPEC Contact Centre (Lumen Books)	36
1982	Lumen Religious Books Trust	36
1983	Women in Theology	A
1984	Catholic Women's Network	
1986	St Joan's International Alliance	36
1987	Women's Ad Hoc Group	
1987	Association for Inclusive Language	E 36
1989	Association of Pastoral Workers	

APPENDIX B

Main characteristics of the feminist network active in the Catholic Church of England and Wales and their respective organisations.

Organisations suffixed '36' are wholly or partly run from 36 Court Lane, Dulwich.

Area of interest	Organisation	
Network co-ordination	The Pastoral Development Group	36
Feminist Literature	Lumen Books (imported from US)	36
Alternative Liturgies	Christian Women's Resource Centre	36
Non-sexist liturgy	Assoc. for Inclusive Language	36
Theology	Newman Theological Studies Group	36
Family (and feminism)	Newman Assoc. Family Committee	36
Anti-*Humanae Vitae*	Catholic Renewal Movement (feminist research interests)	36
Political	Christian Organisations for Social Political and Econcomic Change (Contact Centre)	36
Women Priests	St Joan's International Alliance	36
Married Priests	Movement for the Ordination of Married Men	
Women's Rights (in the Church)	Catholic Women's Network Association for Pastoral Workers	
Homosexual Rights	Catholic Lesbian Sisterhood	
Militant Feminists	Roman Catholic Feminists (Dorcas Group)	
Holidays	Catholic People's Weeks	
Network meetings	Women's Ad Hoc Group (Heythrop)	
Main spheres of influence	National Board of Catholic Women Newman Association Catholic Renewal Movement *The Catholic Herald* *The Tablet*	
Academic base	London University (Extra Mural Studies)	

THE ENEMY WITHIN

Other groups connected and in sympathy with the Catholic feminist network:
   Christian Women's Information
   and Resource Centre
   Movement for the Ordination of Women
   One for Christian Renewal
   Feminist Theology Project
   Christian Parity Group
   Urban Theology Unit
   Women in Theology

Two:

Christian Feminism: The Heresy of the Age

William Oddie

Over 40 years ago, C S Lewis wrote an article explaining why – as it seemed to him – it was highly unlikely the Church of England would ever ordain women to its priesthood. Writing within the Anglo-Catholic tradition, he saw the priest as "a double representative, who represents us to God, and God to us". As he usually did, he moved beyond the immediate topic to what lay behind it. "Suppose", he said,

. . . the reformer stops saying that a good woman may be like God, and begins saying that God is like a good women. Suppose he says that we might just as well pray to 'Our Mother which art in heaven' as to 'Our Father'. Suppose he suggests that the Incarnation might just as well have taken a female form as a male form, and the second person of the Trinity as well called the Daughter as the Son . . . All this, as it seems to me, is involved in the claim that a woman can represent God as a priest does.

Now it is surely the case that if . . . these supposals were ever carried into effect we should be embarked on a different religion. Goddesses have, of course, been worshipped: many religions have had priestesses. But they are religions quite different in character from *Christianity* (my italics).

They are, in fact, so different in character from Christianity that to suggest – in the current state of the debate, and given

29

the widespread ignorance of the issues involved – that ordaining Christian women-priests might be part of a radical de-Christianisation of Christianity is to open oneself to misrepresentation, sometimes even to ridicule. Most of those who, when asked, tell polling organisations they support women's ordination have no intention of worshipping God as Mother, and would never dream of introducing God the Mother into the Lord's prayer. Those who think this a remote possibility, however, should reflect on the case of the Anglican Church of New Zealand, which has done precisely that: it has also installed the first Anglican diocesan woman-bishop, a not unconnected event.

In England, campaigns like the Anglican Movement for the Ordination of Women (MOW) have, for the most part, maintained a determinedly non-radical reformist image, especially in such establishment milieux as the Church of England's General Synod. A closer scrutiny of MOW publications, however, – especially those intended for internal consumption – discloses a considerably more radical feminism at the organisation's hard core than it allows to surface in debates staged for the wider public.

What are the underlying theological assumptions of such movements? Just how radical are those who tend to make the running within them? Can we say, for instance, that radical Christian feminism as it has developed since his day bears out C S Lewis's analysis? How close are radical feminists within the Churches – as represented, for instance, within the Roman Catholic Church by militant tendencies like the "Women-Church" movement, and organisations like the St Joan's International Alliance (SJIA) and the Catholic Women's Network (CWN) – to being "embarked on a different religion"?

Certainly, they are more than inclined, like Lewis's "reformer", to say that we might just as well pray to "Our Mother which art in heaven" as to "Our Father". More: they will mostly insist that calling God "Father" is part of a "patriarchal" conceptual system which has established and nurtured the alleged oppression of women within the Christian Church.

The last claim is worth examining, for it is almost universal among Christian feminists. In the words of the Catholic feminist activist Catherina Halles,

> . . . it is hardly possible to call to mind a single feminist theologian, whatever her phase of development may be, who does not find the image of Father-God a challenge and a direct confrontation.

Halles goes on (almost inevitably) to quote the famous battle cry of the matriarchalist pagan-writer Mary Daly: "If God is male, then the male is God". To see God as a Father, that is to say, has confirmed the status quo of "patriarchal" society, and has sacralised the domination of women by men. This domination is reinforced, in this view, by the maleness of the Son, who himself constantly addresses God as Father, and who, in the dominant Christian tradition, has been represented by an exclusively male priesthood.

But, feminists go on to argue – the "maleness" of this "image" of God does not merely *Legitimate* human society's "patriarchal domination" of the female sex: the Fatherhood of God is, in fact, a *product* of this domination, "spawned", says Daly, "in the human imagination". She continues:

> If God in "his" heaven is a father ruling "his" people, then it is in the "nature" of things and according to divine plan and the order of the universe that society be male dominated.

(Daly, once a Roman Catholic, has now moved into a post-Christian phase; her anti-Christian book *Beyond God the Father*, nevertheless, retains a strong influence over feminists within the Church).

There are clear objections to this line of argument. Most obviously, perhaps it is far from clear that matriarchal religions, or religions with a mixed pantheon of gods and goddesses, were ever reflected by a higher position for women in society: there is, in fact, considerable evidence to the contrary. Certainly, matriarchal religions were never mirrored by matriarchal societies (societies, that is, ruled by a female governing caste), and there is no evidence that any such society has ever existed: myths to this effect are not regarded as historically reliable tradition by anthropologists. The societies which worshipped fertility goddesses were, in fact, every bit as patriarchal as the Hebrew society by which some of them were replaced, though the position of women in them was certainly lower.

A more straightforward objection is the lack of any evidence that, either now or in Christian history, women in any significant numbers have felt themselves excluded and oppressed by the perception of God as Father, or have expected their own femaleness to be mirrored in their symbolic understanding of God as an object of worship. Christian feminists, however, have never been deterred by the fact that only a tiny minority of Christian women accept their analysis: this inconvenient fact is explained away by the centuries of supposed conditioning by a patriarchal Church which has made it acceptable to them to pray to a Father God.

The feminist mission, therefore, is to "raise the conscious-ness" of their mentally enslaved sisters: and finding a language for God which reflects a specifically female image and which refuses to accept as definitive the New Testament symbolism of God as Father and as Son is a first priority of Christian feminist theology and liturgical experiment.

Whether this embarks Christian feminism on a voyage beyond the boundaries of Christian revelation into "a new religion" is a question which most Christian leaders in the West (even including many Catholic bishops) prefer to avoid, perhaps nervous of confrontation with an aggressive movement which often convincingly claims far wider support among women in the Church than it actually possesses.

It is becoming increasingly clear, as the evidence accumulates and its implications emerge, that the attempt by feminists to use non-biblical female language for God is – to use unfashionable but unavoidable language – plainly heretical, and that this makes "Christian feminism" itself a heresy in the classical sense. "Christian feminism", that is to say, cannot be seen as a legitimate development *within* the mainstream Christian tradition: rather, it is a development *from* that tradition, and one which moves decisively beyond its boundaries. As the "post-Christian" feminist theologian Daphne Hampson (a veteran of the Anglican campaign to ordain women) put it, writing from years of experience as a Christian feminist and as an ex-Christian still active with organisations like the Catholic Women's Network:

> Nothing would seem to indicate better the incompatibility between feminism and Christianity than the difficulty in naming God in a female way within that tradition. Yet *that they should see God in their own image*, and not in the image of the opposite sex, has become fundamental to many women. (my italics)

To see God "in their own image", of course, is not what Christians have ever done: he is One whose ways are not our ways, nor are his thoughts our thoughts. He in no way reflects our nature, nor does the life of prayer in the Christian tradition aim at the consolidation of our nature as it actually is.

It is, therefore, fundamental to an authentically Christian understanding of the Fatherhood of God, that it is not simply seen as a metaphor referring to human fatherhood. The Fatherhood of God is a reality, it is part of the revelation Christ came to give: we are not dependent, for the reception of this reality, on cultural factors such as a suitable earthly father-figure for purposes of comparison, any more than the efficacy of the Eucharist is dependent on bread or wine of a suitable quality.

To say that "God is our Father" is not a mere human metaphor: it is the same kind of statement as Christ's "this is my body": a symbolic statement, but not one which is *merely* symbolic. For the Christian disciple, there is in the vocative "Our Father" such an identity between the word and the reality that the two cannot be sundered: when a Christian prays the Lord's prayer, there is (to quote Luther's words on the Eucharist) such "a unity of word and deed, of picture and thing" that it can only be broken in the Christian mind by a real loss of contact with a fundamental reality of faith.

Jesus himself is recorded in the gospels as using the word Father – both in addressing God and in talking about Him – some 170 times: it is his name for God, and with only one exception, it is the only word he uses. At no point does Jesus imply that God is merely *like* a Father to him: his message is that in very truth *God actually is his Father*. He is begotten, not made. And this understanding is at the heart of the faith of the early Church. In the words of the great biblical scholars Edwyn Hoskins and Noel Davey "the definition of Jesus as the Son of God, and the consequent rider that God is his Father, underlie all the books of the New Testament. These were the fundamental dogmas of primitive Christian theology and ethics". "Call no man your father on earth", says Jesus, "for you have one Father, who is in heaven" (Matt 23:9). "I bow my knees", says Paul, "before the Father, *from whom all fatherhood in heaven and on earth is named*" (Eph 3:14).

It was Feuerback and Marx, in the nineteenth century, who reversed this understanding, insisting, in effect, that it is from human fatherhood that God the Father is named. In Marx's words "Man makes religion". Religion is not received from God, but invented by humanity to fulfil its own needs: "religion", he pronounced, "is the self-consciouness and self-feeling of man". Marx's formula translates into the feminist idiom with an uncanny accuracy of tone, as "feminist religion is the self-consciousness and the self-feeling of woman". It is important to remember, though, that Marx was describing what he believed to be an illusion to be abolished and not a reality to be embraced, and that Daphne Hampson's phrase "in their own image" appeared first in the Old Testament as part of a story describing the Israelites rejecting the true God and falling into idolatry.

It is in fact, not necessary – given the way in which feminist religion among Christians has actually developed – to prolong the discussion as to whether it is possible to remain true to the Christian scriptures and tradition while acting on the feminist analysis. There are, of course, many feminisms, and it is certainly the case that some feminists in the Church (with considerable strain on their ingenuity) have attempted a biblical feminism. But in practical terms, this effort has now virtually ceased. All we need do is observe.

Perhaps the most representative Christian feminist is the American Catholic writer Rosemary Radford Ruether – representative in two senses of the word, that she accurately indicates the movement's general tendency, and that she would be accepted by most Christian feminists as speaking for them. Hers has been the decisive influence on Christian feminism – second only to that of the post-Christian Mary Daly – both through her writings and through her activism. She has had a strong influence over the Christian feminist movement in England, and particularly within the Catholic Church.

In 1984, she was the main speaker at the launch of the Catholic Women's Network (CWN) at St Mary's College, Strawberry Hill, a Catholic teacher training college (the same year, the SJIA was listed for the first time in the *Catholic Directory*). She spoke at meetings in England in 1986 and 1988; in 1989 she gave the keynote address at a conference (which was to have important results) at Heythrop College, a Catholic institute which is part of London University. This

35

conference was interestingly described as being "for women working within the structures".

It began with an "apple blessing": about 100 women all said together:

> This is the apple of consciousness-raising, let the scales of false consciousness fall from our eyes, so that we can rightly name truth from falsehood, good and evil.

The symbolism here is obvious enough: "false consciousness" is clearly equated with biblical tradition as the Church has received it. The "apple" which Eve in the Genesis story gives to Adam, the eating of which is a dramatic metaphor for the disobedience to God which brought the fall of man, now becomes the symbol of a new religious quest in which God will be made in the image of woman.

Perhaps Ruether's most influential works are *Sexism and God-talk* (1983), *Woman-Guides* (1985) and *Woman-Church* (1986). These last two works were intended as ideological and liturgical resources for a kind of internal Catholic women's sect, called "Woman-Church", which began to spread under Ruether's influence among radical activists in America during the eighties. "Woman-Church" was established in England by two SJIA committee members in 1990 – the year following the Heythrop College meeting, at which the strategies of the movement had been spelt out by Ruether herself in a session entitled "Towards a new vision of the Church".

What exactly do Ruether and her followers mean by "a new vision of the Church"? *Woman-Guides* is a collection of texts, a first contribution to what Ruether sees as a priority for feminists: the displacement of the Bible as the normative source for Christian belief, so that it becomes simply one source among many for what she calls a new textual base, a new canon. "What women should achieve within the Church", she says, "cannot be done from the existing base of the Christian Bible".

Her "textual base" includes material from a wide variety

of sources, including a picture of the Goddess Isis leading Queen Nefertiti by the hand (underneath is the caption "Hand in hand, women guide each other as they claim their buried past and journey to the place of the death of patriarchy and the beginning of new possibilities for womanbeing"). Texts include a psalm addressed to the great Goddess of Babylonia, material relating to the Father/Mother God of Christian Science, and stories of courageous women in the nineteenth century.

To describe Ruether's brand of feminist religion as semi-pagan is not to insult her ideas, but simply to describe them. In her own words:

Feminist spirituality today is reassessing pre-Christian religion. Does a pagan veneration of nature disclose a more ecological relation between humanity and nature? Do myths and cults of Goddesses provide alternative resources for women's identity?

The Christian – and certainly the Catholic – answer to these questions is clear enough. It is not Ruether's; indeed, at one point we find her saying (in *Concilium*, a liberal Catholic journal) that though she has *some* reservations about feminist witchcraft, or Wicca, nevertheless,

. . . it is possible that we are witnessing in this movement the first stirrings of what may become a new stage of human religious consciousness.

Ruether's ideas were expounded in a lecture delivered by this pre-eminent feminist heroine and guru in the hall of Westminster Cathedral – the very centre of English Catholicism – in 1986, and significantly entitled "Is there a place for feminists in the Christian Church?". The answer of many religious feminists to this question is an emphatic negative. The theologian Daphne Hampson, a veteran of the Anglican campaign to ordain women, is one former Christian no longer prepared to stay in a religion in which God is Father, Son and Holy Spirit.

37

The fact is, however, that the overwhelming majority of Christian women are perfectly happy to worship God the Father, and have perceived without difficulty that feminist religious ideas are the most unmitigated nonsense. Quite simply feminists do not speak for most women. Why, then, should anybody worry?

The answer is that Ruether and her followers are not prepared to leave, and that they intend to change the Church from within, if necessary by stealth. As she put it in the newsletter of the CWN:

> We should use the institutional resources that have disempowered women to re-empower women.

This is the strategy already being successfully followed by the firmly Ruetherite organisations CWN and SJIA, which are now highly influential constituent members of the National Board of Catholic Women, an organisation officially described as "a consultative body to the Catholic Bishops' Conference". They have received effective backing from powerful individuals in the hierarchy's supporting bureaucracy – that is, "within the structures".

One of their first achievements as members of the Board was to persuade it to agree to compiling a radical "report" on the alleged oppression of women in the Church, supposedly representing the views of the Catholic women's organisations which are affiliated to the Board. In fact, these bodies were not given a chance either to endorse or to repudiate the report before it was published, and those which protested after the event have been simply ignored. The report was sent to the Catholic Bishops of England and Wales with the Board's authority, and represented to them as reflecting the discontent of ordinary Catholic women. This particular operation, which must rank as one of the most successful examples of entryism since the hard left nearly took over the labour party, originated among the fifty members of the Saint Joan's International Alliance, which at that time appeared in the *Catholic Directory* as an organisation which has "ecclesiastical approval".

Similar stories can be told of activist feminist encroachments in other Churches, which (not having the ultimate safeguard of the Catholic Magisterium) are even more vulnerable to the effects of such activities. The Catholic Church will survive this latest blast of heretical doctrine, as it has survived such assaults in every generation; the guardians of the deposit of faith, the bishops, will in the end perceive the feminist challenge for what it is and act accordingly.

The danger until they do is not for the survival of the Church itself, but for the individual souls who are always the chief casualty during periods of uncertainty about the Church's teaching. For other Churches and ecclesial groups, this present turmoil may well be part of a process of terminal decline: perhaps the clearest example of this is the rapidly disappearing Episcopal Church of the USA, whose survival as an identifiably Christian organisation is now increasingly doubtful.

The least that needs to be understood is that radical feminism represents in this generation a major danger to the mission of the Church; and that this threat always presents itself when the Church is less than clear about what its tradition teaches. The present attack is directed particularly at the authority of Holy Scripture; Christians of all persuasions might with profit pray together in Archbishop Thomas Cranmer's words:

> *Give us grace, that, being not like children carried away with every blast and vain doctrine, we may be established in the truth of the holy Gospel; through Jesus Christ our Lord.*

Three:

Women's Rites

Feminist Liturgies and the Catholic Tradition

Josephine Robinson

The urge to worship is among the deepest instincts of man. It subsumes a recognition that man has limits and has been made by a higher power. Man, from the first, knows the truth of this and worships.

From earliest times, anthropologists tell us, this instinct was expressed sometimes spontaneously, sometimes in an ordered and symbolic manner. Man (as humankind) first recognised that the food he needed was not produced by himself. It was not he, himself, who caused the seed to sprout, the blade to grow. Men and women recognised that rain and sun did not originate in them. They became aware of the recurrence, through the passing seasons, of a fundamental pattern of yearly renewal, and allied themselves with the power of vegetation, or the powers behind vegetation. The very early rites, like that of Eleusis, which involved cutting the corn in silence, may be seen as a simple thanksgiving. There are also many "Ascension" rites found in pastoral and hunting cultures, which take account of fecundity and death. Life is seen to feed on death.

Indeed the meal is another frequent theme, seen as uniting mankind with the Creative Power, or with a past or future land of happiness and fulfilment. In the beginning, man feels he acts only within divine action. At a later stage, he sees his act as magic – that is, making God or gods do something in accordance with the will of man. In

40

petitionary prayer, mankind acknowledges God as supreme and humbly asks favour. According to Louis Bouyer, in the case of magic, God is seen as being tricked or forced into some action by man. Magic is, therefore, not primitive, but calculated.[1] In primitive society, the whole of reality is considered sacred. The relationship between mankind and the divine is one and indivisible, the dependency total, the wonder at the God-given cycle of seed, blade and full ear of wheat, ever present. Later, when man comes to self-awareness, he keeps some space for himself, excluding the divine. The further he extends his space, the less is his interest in the Deity. Then rites are seen as making something sacred (whereas they present something sacred) or as averting evil by constraining the Almighty. When, later still,

> Man loses the faith that animated his rituals and especially his sacrifices, he comes to regret the loss . . . he misses the emotion and the feelings of exaltation . . . associated with it. He then seeks, either by reviving the past or instituting new techniques, to recover something of that psychological atmosphere which surrounded them, without giving credence to the original beliefs.[2]

It is at this point that feelings become all important and religiosity is substituted for religion; atheists express a love of Choral Evensong and humanists dwell on plain chant. Nevertheless a sense of mystery can transform ordinary feelings and the response to it is deeply human. If we see myth, not as fiction, but as an attempt to express and understand the human condition, then we can see prayer as a way from myth to the Divine.

These cries from the heart are strongly exemplified in the Psalms, which form, as it were, a gateway into the worship of the Church. They are rooted in the immediate concerns of the people, but carry these concerns directly to Yahweh, with a strong, fervent feeling of dependence.

41

Tell me Yahweh when my end will be,
How many days are allowed me
Show me how frail I am.[3]

I waited and waited for Yahweh
Now at last he has stooped to me
And heard my cry for help.[4]

Save me God! The water
Is already up to my neck.[5]

Psalms have from the first formed part of Christian liturgies, expressing as they do faith and hope in the Lord.

When we consider feminist liturgies, we find the essentials of worship are changed. We find, in many cases, that the space is kept for the participants and that praise and worship is not offered to the God of Christianity. Christians worship a transcendent God, creator and sustainer of all that is:

Giver of breath and bread
World's strand, sway of the sea
Lord of the living and dead.
. . . tho' he is under the world's splendour and wonder
His mystery must be instressed, stressed.[6]

He is above, beneath, beyond His creation. Out of His transcendence and benevolence, He asks us to call Him Father.

Feminists, in their liturgies, do not, on the whole, direct their prayer to God the Father, through His Son. In the *Rite of Healing for Wife-Battering*, the Presider says:

We have cried out to the God of our Fathers, but we have not been heard . . . We must strip off the masks of patriarchy . . .[7]

In a version of the Lord's Prayer given in *Woman-created Liturgies* God is addressed as

Eternal Spirit, life-giver, pain-bearer, love-maker, source of all that is and that shall be, Father and Mother of us all, Loving God, in whom is heaven.[8]

I think Our Lord put it better.

They invoke Holy Wisdom, Great Mother and Father, the Mother Spirit. "Feminine" aspects of God become paramount, God immanent in His creation is stressed, seen as a well-spring of human life. The androgynous God, Father and Mother of us all, points the way to the worship of a goddess. Homage is turned from the active God, creator and redeemer, to God-in-creation "Loving God in whom is heaven",[9] something the early Gnostic sects would have recognised:

Come, she who knows the secret of the elect
. . . Come and partake with us of this Eucharist
which we celebrate in your name
. . . to which we have gathered at your behest.[10]

This liturgy actually comes from the *Acts of Thomas* written in the third century: it would fit neatly into contemporary women's liturgies. As in the liturgies we are considering, human beings, not God, hold centre stage.

In the *Rite of Reconciliation and Passage for the Dying* the Speaker is to say:

All the goodness of doing and being is in your life gathered here together into one . . . and offered up to the Mother-Spirit, the source of all life, who will take it back into herself and make it immortal and everlasting.[11]

Women's liturgies divide the people of God.

The Eucharist is for everybody, men and women, old and young, learned and simple, once they can distinguish between ordinary bread and the consecrated host. Catholics believe that at every Mass Christ offers himself sacramentally on the Cross for our sins, gives himself to us to be the food of our souls. Within the Catholic family, only those who have put themselves outside the Church by serious, unrepented sin are denied Communion, though not attendance at Mass. All are joined at the Lord's table.

There is little mention of the Mass in feminist writings.

The "Eucharistic celebrations" they describe bear only a passing resemblance to the sacramental re-enactment of the Crucifixion of Our Lord, acted out, as the *Catechism of Christian Doctrine* says "In an unbloody manner"[12] on the altar. Indeed Dr Reuther is quoted as saying during her visit to London in 1988 that,

. . . the point about the Sacraments is not what happens to the bread and wine, but what happens to us.[13]

That statement is, of course, very far from the teaching of the Church on the Sacraments. They are actions of Christ himself, not rites of passage or means of inducing certain moods or feelings. Without sacramental reality, rooted in Christ, we would have only the memories of Our Lord's life on earth and whatever we could perceive of the Holy Spirit within us. The grace brought to us by the Sacraments is the life-giving gift of God Himself, freeing us from the bondage of original sin, granting us forgiveness and reconciling us after personal sin, strengthening us, endowing marriage with the vital spark of love, answering our needs in sickness and health. Our Lord's gift of himself under the appearances of bread and wine is unique.

Rosemary Radford Reuther is none-the-less reported as saying that women need to re-appropriate sacramental life, that original sin is the inheritance of structures of oppression and conversion is escaping them.[14]

Instead of seeing unjust discrimination, whether sexual, racial or in any other sphere as part of our failure to love our neighbour as ourself, radical feminists present the oppression of women, real or imagined, as the only sin.

In a "Garden Liturgy" in *Women Created Liturgies* there is a Celebrant who shares some of *her* experiences with us, followed by a litany in which men and women alternately ask to be freed from

Playing the passive role in which society casts us (women), from taking sexism less seriously than racism (men), from

44

thinking in stereotypes rather than seeing each human as unique (all).[15]

The author's stereotyping seems to have escaped her notice. A comment on the closing prayer, which is

All Eternal God, heavenly father, you have graciously accepted us as loving members of your Son . . .[16]

reads: "Note the date when this was written – 1983 – today we would not use this phraseology in an inclusive liturgy." The language of the Bible is to be abandoned.

In another Eucharistic Liturgy called *Feminine Aspects of the Triune God, Creator, Redeemer and Spirit*[17], we find a prolix penitential rite, which talks of failure, not sin – it is, of course, true that all sin is failure, but not all failure is sin. Then, after short readings, a few lines from Genesis, Deuteronomy and Hosea, there are a mere three lines from St Matthew, expressive of God's love for His people. In place of a homily, there is a question and answer session with pencil and paper. "You have approximately 25 minutes" it threatens. While they are sharpening their pencils, the "Leader" gives them "Discussion Points". In the characteristic style of radical feminist polemic, these are that God the Father is not male in the sense of being of the masculine gender (quite right, though they omit to remark that He is a Spirit). They then claim that the "establishment argument" that women cannot be ordained to the ministerial priesthood means that his male gender is more "important than the many feminine qualities that Christ exhibited".

The questions themselves are clearly loaded and the respondents are expected to answer that Jesus showed "feminine" characteristics and that therefore women can represent him at the altar.

The *Our Father*, recited before the Consecration begins "Lord God, far above our understanding, father and mother of us all", is followed by the Eucharistic prayer which everyone is supposed to recite together and which is not too far distant from the words of the Mass. What status we are supposed to accord to the elements thus prayed over is unclear. The intention of those who compiled this liturgy is difficult to determine. The authors state:

There will be a basket of bread for the young children and anyone else who will not be going to communion . . .

So they see a difference between "blessed bread" and bread consecrated by the female Leader and everyone else.[18]

A do-it-yourself element is much favoured in women's liturgies. In a "Palm Sunday Rite", written by Peter Kettle for the St Hilda's Community "each turns to their neighbour (sic) and gives absolution".[19] Here, the priesthood of the people of God is distorted into superseding the ordained ministry, which is strange when the author seems to want this priesthood for women! He makes it appear hardly worth having.

The readings in the Palm Sunday Rite are headed "Women of the Passion", including, of course, the anointing at Bethany – a central text of women's liturgies. The readings are again followed by discussion in groups – surely misplaced within liturgical action, for that is a time for praying to God, not arguing with each other.

Under the heading "Do this in commemoration of me", two suggestions for prayer are made. The first reads:

Eternal Wisdom, we praise you and give you thanks, because you laid aside your power as a garment . . .
You became obedient unto death, even death on a cross, receiving authority and comfort from the hands of a woman . . .[20]

That is an astounding statement for any Christian to make. Jesus made it plain in St John's Gospel when he prayed "Father the hour has come, glorify your Son so that your Son may glorify you"[21] that his authority came from the Father. Does the author intend to suggest that Mary of Bethany gave authority to Jesus by anointing him with oil?

Anointing is a favourite action in women's liturgies, sometimes to rather comic effect. There is no biblical justification for this. Jesus himself said, "She has done it for my burial".[22]

The second suggestion follows the do-it-yourself theme of the earlier mutual absolution. This time we read "now let us take this bread and break and share it in the name of Christ".[23]

A less positive view of the Eucharist is expressed by Rosemary Radford Reuther. She states her belief that women need to "re-appropriate" ministry from the clergy, who have made it a thing "they alone" can do.[24] She wants the Eucharist to be an expression of women's struggle for "empowerment". Thanksgiving has no part in it, let alone re-enactment of the redemptive sacrifice of Christ on Calvary and his gift of himself at the Last Supper.

Alexina Murphy, of the Catholic Women's Network, wrote in their Newsletter that they are now ready

> to offer women an alternative celebration of the central mysteries of our faith, using women's experience as our resource to create liturgy.[25]

Rituals can generate strong emotions, can swing moods and induce feelings and even actions that may be inappropriate among the group. They need, therefore, to be strongly controlled and the emotion channelled towards God, so that it is helpful, not destructive.

The Rites set out in *Woman-Church* by Rosemary Radford Reuther, the best-known handbook of women's liturgies, prey on the feelings and seem to aim at quasi-hypnotic effects. They are so unlike the tradition of worship in the Catholic Church that one is tempted to echo Jane Austen's Mr Bingley in his reply to his sister's remark that rational conversation rather than dancing should be the order of a ball. "Much more rational, my dear Caroline, I daresay, but not near so much like a ball". Much more up-to-date, I daresay, but not near so much like a Mass.

Radford Reuther's church is circular. What moves her is the oppression (sometimes, indeed, real) of women. Her liturgies reflect this limited concern, constantly turning back on themselves, never liberating their spirit towards God. The anger she projects constantly swings round to fan its own flame.

In her introduction to *Woman-Church*, she writes that the

. . . feminist religious revolution promises to be more radical and far-reaching then liberation theologies. It goes behind the symbolic universe that has been constructed by patriarchal civilization.[26]

In short, everything we recognise as being part of the Christian inheritance is rejected. She goes on to remark that

. . . recognition of our need for prayer and ritual is shared not only by Christian feminists but by those who seek to revive the old religion of the Goddesses . . . Catholic women are beginning to recognise the need for autonomous bases for women's theologizing and worship . . . Woman-Church is rooted in 'creation-based spirituality'.

This means that the grace of redemptive life is not beyond nature.[27]

In the most developed, or most extreme women's liturgies we find a religion of nature, not grace, with divine powers invested in the earth – in spite, one might have thought, of every scrap of evidence. We are looking at the religion of the goddess. Interestingly, though many feminists dislike and protest at the male connotation of God the Father, they are quite happy to worship a goddess. We must assume that they reject the idea of fatherhood and wish to dissociate themselves from men.

Rosemary Radford Reuther's "Woman-Church" is circular because it looks continually at the women who are supposed to form it. Who these women would be is a matter for speculation. On internal evidence, they would appear to have unlimited time and a taste for amateur dramatics. Above all, they devote their energies to prolonged consideration of the wrongs they and other women have suffered. Although the author admits that most women who perform these ceremonies, will meet in each others houses she describes the architecture of "Woman-Church" in some detail. The building envisaged would be something between a health club and a conference centre, containing in addition to a large circular room, lit by a windowed dome for liturgies, conferences and collective meals, a round crypt for "rites connected with birth and death". An egg-shaped building (for conversation) would be divided by an indoor garden, from another area containing a "hot tub, a cool plunge, saunas, steam baths and toilets". Warming to her theme she says the garden would be planted with roses and herbs for healing and "bracing teas". The setting would be woodland and it would have several small cottages scattered about, with sleeping and creating areas where women could stay for some days to meditate, read and write. She advocates the use of such cottages for women menstruating.[28]

The liturgy *Reclaiming Menstruation* is one of the most characteristic. The rubric states, "Women gather in a circle with a lighted green candle and a red candle for each woman".[29] There is also a bowl for each one and a ball of red yarn. The candles symbolise the new life and the "dying egg". The hen's eggs symbolise the eggs "that are born in our bodies each month",[30] she writes, with a fine disregard for biological fact. The red yarn links the women together in a circle. They say together:

> We are the circle of the mothers, the life-bearers. This yarn is the stream of power that unites us with each other, with all women and with all the powers of the universe.[31]

What powers, one wonders, does she have in mind? One would have hoped that mothers would be united with their husbands in the God-given unity of marriage, two in one flesh. But no.

Having spent some time telling stories of their monthly cycles, the women are to strip off and bathe with ritual movements in a convenient pool of water, saying "Blessed is the dying away and blessed the regeneration".[32] Then they emerge together from the water and clothe themselves in "bright robes of new cloth".[33] This statement highlights the absurdity of this proceeding. There is also something unpleasantly sentimental in the tale-telling and the ritual dip. There is nothing Christian about it, the "power of the universe" being undefined. The "stream of power" spoken of has nothing to do with the grace of God which transforms believers. There is no thanking God for the fashioning of women, body and soul, for their capacity to bear children; no asking a blessing on the love between husband and wife; no prayer to Mary, Theotokos, who as both virgin and mother is the model for all women, to ask her to intercede for us.

Practical difficulties apart, a liturgy of that sort would surely have a very limited appeal. But what are we to make of the hugs and anointings which occur in many liturgies and even in the Mass itself? Bishops anoint in Confirmation and Holy Orders, priests in giving the Sacrament of the Sick. Kings are anointed, as an admission that their power is subject to a higher one. The woman of Bethany anointed Jesus, out of love, not power.[34] Feminists would seem to lean towards power rather than sympathy.

In many women's liturgies, "victims" are urged to tell their story. Story-telling is a frequently used technique. Confessional stories raise anger; they tempt the teller to self-pity, the listener to sympathetic rage. Whether or not they are therapeutic is an open question and would, in any case, depend on the skill of the therapist. Otherwise the surge of emotion can even be damaging.

In the "Liturgy of Healing for a Battered Wife", women

and men stand in a circle. The "Presider" says that under patriarchy marriage has

. . . too often been a licence for legalized violence against women . . . A theology of victimisation turns the crucifixion of Christ into a spirituality of sadism for men and masochism for women.[35]

That is a statement that must be rebutted by all Christians. It is a parody of the theology of Christ's perfect self-giving in love. There follows a prayer which "integrates Psalm 22 with a letter from a battered wife". Alternate groups recite the story and psalm antiphonally. The author remarks that

. . . the male language of the psalm is retained as an expression of the ambivalent recourse a patriarchal God presents for women subjected to violence.[36]

"We must strip off the masks of patriarchy from our God and Goddess"[37] says the presider in a "reflection prayer". The woman tells her story, and several women anoint parts of her body with perfumed ointment, saying, "This (hand, face, chest, back, leg) was created to feel and enjoy life".[38] After this theologically inadequate statement, they cry "Be healed". They do not ask God to heal the woman, as Jesus healed the woman with the issue of blood. They do not ask Our Lady to intercede for her. They do not pray that the battering husband will turn his back on his sins of violence.

We find Dr Reuther describing Baptism as the "exorcism of patriarchy" in the "Rite of Mind-Cleansing from the Pollution of Sexism", using a broken pen to represent those women who were willing to discard their

. . . aspirations for careers and education because they accepted the message that women's place is in the home . . . [39]

as if a happy family and small children brought up in close contact with their mothers was not one of the greatest blessings that can be bestowed upon us.

51

Since antipathy, hostility and envy (penis envy, in Freud's terminology) of men is expressed in many of the liturgies of "Woman-Church", it is not surprising that lesbian relationships loom large in these liturgies. In "Coming Out Rite for a Lesbian", baptismal traditions are milked (if one may use the metaphor) and the words of the psalmist are employed for a purpose from which he would have recoiled in horror.

Where would I go to escape your spirit?
Where would I flee from your presence? . . .
I thank you for the wonder of myself,
for the wonder of your works.[40]

The celebrant and other friends pour or sprinkle water with words such as these:

Born of woman, beloved of woman, lover of woman
You are blessed
You are the light of the world.[41]

Wheadon United Methodist Church in Evanston, Illinois witnessed a "Covenant Celebration for a Lesbian Couple". It featured a call to awareness:

You are the people who have been family for us. We rejoice that you have come to witness our beginning in our new family.[42]

A prayer of Confession reads "We confess that we have all faltered on our journey to the New Earth". A reading from the Book of Ruth puts forward an interpretation that would have dismayed The Old Testament writer, as it does Christians today. Rings are exchanged with words of excruciating coyness and sentimentality:

I give this ring to you: it represents tears running, turning sideways into laughter.[43]

The two women finally claim a joint name for themselves: "Kinheart . . . the name for ourselves in relationship". The Communion Song 'Take and Eat' is sung as water, raisins, grapes and bread are passed around.

At a more innocuous level, Dr Reuther has a "Ritual of Moving from an Old House to New House".[44] It is nevertheless a good example of her florid, not to say Turkey Carpet, style of ritualizing. Anyone who has ever moved house knows that it is not a time for gathering friends around and invoking good spirits of each room (even if we acknowledge their existence) for burning incense and scattering grain about. But what a good moment for a quick prayer of thanks to God who shelters us, a prayer for all the families involved in this and other moves, a prayer to Our Lady, who knew all about moving house, as a refugee, with a donkey instead of a removal van, and with the most precious burden of the Holy Child. A prayer to St Joseph, the selfless guardian of them both, asking him to pray that the new house will have a place for Christ within it, would make good sense.

Dr Reuther may be considered the high priestess of these sickly rites. But what are we to make of Brid Fitzpatrick's "Impressions: Women Celebrate Death and New Life" during Holy Week.[45] A web of different coloured ribbons "weaving in our joys and sorrows, weaknesses and strengths" was spread on the floor on Holy Thursday. The participants joined hands to bless bread and wine before it was shared. There is no mention in the account, that the participants also attended the Mass of the Last Supper, so we must assume that Catholic women chose this rather than joining with the Universal Church, women and men, in celebration of the New Commandment.

Then they had a "roly-poly session" in which women gave each other "bear hugs", "rolling over and over with much wild shrieking and giggling. Women on their hands and knees side by side with another woman lying on their gently swaying backs. Women swaying backward, caught and tenderly held, then lifted high and lowered again – learning letting go and trust".[46]

On Good Friday, they followed up these unseemly goings on by remembering the earth as mother.

On Saturday, they took a tip from the Church's Liturgy and began their rites in darkness. "Then Mary Magdalene meets Christ and is charged with a mission . . . stirring music"[47] We are told that God is revealed in the faces and voices of women. They celebrate their strength and the empowerment that comes from devising their own liturgies.

Whatever qualms Catholics may have about contemporary translations from the Bible, they can be confident that they never reach depths of banality to match that of the liturgy reported in this Newsletter. Their Eucharist was a large chocolate cake, which they decorated with smarties to represent "something we wished for the world".[48]

In *Celebrating Women*,[49] a punning title, illustrated by a parody of Michelangelo's painting of God the Father touching Adam's finger, which shows two female figures in the same pose, a "Wilderness Liturgy" alters Bunyan's Hymn so that it reads "If she with giants fight" – something, perhaps, small feminists, however ardent, might prefer to leave unchanged from the original. God is thanked for the women's "foremothers". They are names such as Miriam, Deborah and Rachel and from the New Testament, the woman of Bethany and Mary Magdalene, "first apostle of the Resurrection".[50]

Much is made in feminist writings of Mary Magdalene and who can quarrel with that? There is no doubt that she was given a great grace in her meeting with the risen Lord and in the instruction she received to break the good news to the Apostles.

The word apostle comes from the Greek Apostellein, meaning to send. Mary Magdalene was sent, therefore she was an apostle, the reasoning goes. But the Church uses the word apostle to designate the Twelve, specially chosen by Christ, and St Paul refers to himself as "being appointed by God to be an apostle".[51]

But, just as there is the priesthood of the people of God, which is distinct from the ordained priesthood, although it shares some of the same characteristics, so there is the Apostleship of all Christians and in that sense St Mary Magdalene is one of the greatest. There is no scriptural evidence for the inference in feminist thinking that she is a portent of the ordination of women to the ministerial priesthood.

The most striking omission from this list of women for whom the liturgy gives thanks is that of the Blessed Virgin Mary. She, whose "yes" to God the Father brought Christ into the world, whose womb sheltered and nurtured him for nine months, who bore him and brought him up. She it was who taught him his prayers, told him the history of the Chosen people. It was at her request that he worked his first miracle. She was with him at the foot of the cross. The highest order of human nature is embedded in her generosity. Surely, of all women she must be our avatar and guide.

Yet Dr Reuther has written:

> I could not tell her (a nun) that my devotion to Mary was somewhat less than my devotion to some more powerful females that I know, Isis, Athena, Artemis.[52]

She reduces Mary to myth and then rejects her.

It seems that for radical feminists her humility obscures her perfect freedom. The Catholic Church teaches that she was born without that pull towards evil which is the result of original sin, but nevertheless, she had a free choice to make. The poet Stevie Smith wrote, "If I had been the Virgin Mary I would have said no". But Mary knew that she was offered this glory and responsibility by God. She did not complain, she did not feel herself ill-used – quite the reverse. In the Gospels only two questions of hers are recorded. She asked the Angel how her motherhood was to be accomplished.[53] She also asked Jesus, when, after three days search they found him, "Why have you done this to us?"

and he replied, "Did you [in the sense of 'even you'] not know that I must be busy with my Father's affairs?"[54]

She did not feel herself marginalized; she did not try to set herself over St Peter who showed plenty of human weakness; she did not even, like St Paul, list her sufferings. She could say "He that is mighty has done great things for me. Holy is his name".[55]

Where Our Lady is mentioned at all, it tends to be in the context of the Magnificat, where she is seen as a symbol of political change. In the "Liturgy of Mary of the Magnificat" a quotation from the feminist theologian Catherina Halles reads that Our Lady's words are

> . . . a prelude in radical subversive language to St Luke's sermon on the plain . . . the last shall be be first and the first last . . . [56]

Radical the Magnificat undoubtedly is but its radicalism is of the spirit. When we remember Christ's dismissal of political issues:

> Give back to Caesar what belongs to Caesar's and to God what belongs to God.[57]

we cannot drag Mary's thinking away from his.

Alongside her supposed "political" role, we find an attempt to cut her down to size, to stress her "ordinariness". She "worried about her son, following him even to the foot of the cross, as any mother would do".[58] But God chose her, not an identikit woman, an everywoman. The emphasis is misplaced. She was indeed a woman of the people. All actors in the accounts of the life of Christ on earth were poor people and it may be that their material poverty enhanced their receptiveness to the Word made Flesh. One of the few whom we see turning away from Christ during his ministry did so because "he was very rich".[59] But her social position hardly matters in the face of her cry "He that is mighty has done great things for me; holy is his name".[60] Before the concluding prayer "All move round the table, link hands and sing a blessing of the food'', all the participants are to say:

> O loving and sustaining Spirit, inspire us to free the image of Mary, Mother of God, from the pious distortions of the ages, and find in her a model of challenge and hope.[61]

Admittedly, Our Lady is sometimes made to look sugary and insipid in plaster statues, but the intention is surely to present her giving of herself and acceptance of us. There is no distortion in that. One fears that the challenge and hope refers to the empowerment of women, not to the love of God.

Feminist liturgies use "inclusive language" no matter how awkward this usage. The writers somehow fail to see the additional richness for women in having a separate word for the female gender as well as the strong common word "man" for all humanity.

This concern is of a very recent origin, it divides the sexes, instead of affirming their common humanity. In English, the word "man" has from the time of the Old English epic Beowulf, had both genetic and individual male meanings. When she was asked if the word person or human could replace man in all contexts, Dr Scorsone, the woman Director of the Toronto Family Life Office replied:

> Only imperfectly. Person has legal and role overtones. Human suggests distinction from animal or alien species. As for man, the context in English is very important and clarifies its meaning adequately, thus "when nature is violated man is the loser" or "God and man at table sat down". Man here includes woman. To enfeeble a language as old and rich as English is to lose a culture. (She goes on) I am a feminist woman and many of us refuse to allow other feminists to exclude us from the word man, to which we have as much right as do men. We refuse to be excluded from 1500 years of English literature. We refuse the rage wished into us by a political agenda. We love our language and have enough problems without this artificial one.[62]

Latin, of course, has two words, *homo* (the species) and *vir*

57

(the male). No-one could argue that this fact improved the standing of Roman women, where in some periods husbands and fathers had rights of life and death over their wives and daughters.

In liturgies and in translating the word of God, inclusive language uses mutually excluding words, like men and women. Ironically enough, man is the inclusive word! Church leaders should surely explain this, and not trade in the insights of long ages for a very superficial political slogan.

"Jesus taught us to call God our Father" says the introduction to the Lord's prayer in the Mass. Jesus called him Father (even Daddy – Abba is a child's word). The Church is the guardian of Christ's teaching and must continue to pray to Our Father, not Our Parent. "Parent" describes a function, not a fact.

"Where two or three are gathered together in my name there am I in the midst of them" said Jesus. It is good for groups of women, groups of men, people in industry, in offices, in the professions, single women, mothers, bachelors, fathers, young and old to pray together as occasion offers, touching on concerns common to them. Such prayer should never become a substitute for the Mass and the sacraments: it must reflect the mind of the Church. Almighty God must be the centre and goal of all our prayer and personal or group concerns should never usurp His place. We have great riches to explore in the Old and New Testaments and the example of the saints. The liturgies I have described and many others seem to go in a different direction.

In his paper "An Ever Reforming Church" given at the XI Meeting for Friendship among Peoples at Rimini in 1991, Cardinal Josef Ratzinger said:

> It can happen that a person is continually active in ecclesiastical associations and activities, but he may not be a Christian at all. It can also happen that a person simply lives only by the word and the Sacraments and puts love

that comes from faith into practice, without ever sitting on an ecclesiastical committee, without ever bothering about the latest in ecclesiastical politics, without ever participating in Synods or voting at them. And yet, he is a true Christian. We do not need a more human Church but a more divine one, only then will it be truly human.[63]

That is where women's liturgies fail.

REFERENCES

1. Louis Bouyer, *Rite and Mankind*, Indiana, University of Notre Dame Press, 1963.
2. *Ibid.*
3. Psalm 39, *Jerusalem Bible*, Darton, Longman and Todd, 1968
4. Psalm 40, *Ibid.*
5. Psalm 69, *Ibid.*
6. Gerard Manley Hopkins, *The Wreck of the Deutschland*, "Collected Poems", Oxford University Press, 1948.
7. R Radford Reuther, *Woman Church*, "The Theory and Practice of Feminist Liturgical Communities", San Francisco, Harper and Row, 1985.
8. *Women Created Liturgies*, Christian Women's Resource Centre, 36 Court Lane, London, SE 21.
9. *Ibid.*
10. Quoted in: Manfred Hauke, *Women in the Priesthood*, San Francisco, Ignatius Press, 1988.
11. R R Reuther, *op., cit.*
12. *Catechism of Christian Doctrine*, revised, London, Catholic Truth Society, 1971.
13. *Catholic Women's Network Newsletter*, 1991
14. *Ibid.* 15. Christian Women's Resource Centre, *op., cit.*
16. *Ibid.*
17. *Ibid.*
18. *Ibid.*
    Note: "Blessed bread", the eulogiae, i.e. blessed by the priest during the Offertory – intended as something anyone could receive – survives occasionally in France (the writer encountered it for the first time in the summer of 1991, near Rouen) and in some Eastern liturgies. The point here is that this liturgy distinguishes between "consecrated", by the women participants, and the "blessed" bread.
19. Peter Kettle, for Association for Inclusive Language, 36 Court Lane, London, SE26.
20. *Ibid.*
21. John 17:1-3, *Jerusalem Bible*.
22. *Ibid.*
23. Peter Kettle, *op., cit.*
24. R R Reuther, *The Tablet*, London, 1989
25. Alexina Murphy, *Catholic Women's Network Newsletter*, September, 1990.
26. Reuther, *op., cit.*
27. *Op., cit.*

28. *Op., cit.*
29. *Op., cit.*
30. *Op., cit.*
31. *Op., cit.*
32. *Op., cit.*
33. *Op., cit.*
34. Mark 14:3-9, *Jerusalem Bible.*
35. Del Martin, *Battered Wives*, San Francisco, Glide Publications, 1976
36. *Ibid.*
37. *Ibid.*
38. *Ibid.*
39. *Ibid.*
40. Rebecca Parker and Jane Brown, "Coming Out Rite for a Lesbian", quoted in R R Reuther, *op., cit.*
41. *Ibid.*
42. Wheadon United Methodist Church, "Covenant Celebration for a Lesbian Couple", quoted in R R Reuther, *op., cit.*
43. *Ibid.*
44. R R Reuther, *op., cit.*
45. Brid Fitzpatrick, "Impressions: Women Celebrate Death and New Life", *Catholic Women's Network Newsletter*, June, 1990.
46. *Ibid.*
47. *Ibid.*
48. Gill Sharpe, *Catholic Women's Network Newsletter*, March, 1991.
49. Janet Morley and Hannah Ward, ed., "Celebrating Women", *Women in Theology*, Movement for the Ordination of Women, 1986.
50. *Ibid.*
51. I Corinthians 1:1, *Jerusalem Bible.*
52. R R Reuther, *Christian Action Journal*, Spring, 1982.
53. Luke 1:34, *Jerusalem Bible.*
54. *Ibid.*, 2:48.
55. *Ibid.*, 1:49.
56. St Joan's International Alliance, *Women Language and the Church*, Association for Inclusive Language, *op., cit.*
57. Matthew 19:20, *Jerusalem Bible.*
58. St Joan's International Alliance, *op., cit.*
59. Matthew 19:20, *op., cit.*
60. Luke 1:20, *op. cit.*
61. St Joan's International Alliance, *op., cit.*
62. Dr Scorsone, *Catholic Clergy Magazine*, USA, 1991.
63. Cardinal Joseph Ratzinger, 'An Ever Reforming Church', *30 Days*, Rome, Instituto Internationale, December 1990.

Four:

Isis and the Crisis of Morality

Cornelia Ferreira

The feminist movement, initiated by Christian women a century ago, embodies two crises in Christian society: a crisis of faith and a crisis of morality. The first chapter of the Epistle to the Romans shows clearly that Christian morality is rooted in faith, and the rejection of God and the truths of creation leads to a rejection of the very nature of man as created by God. This results in sins against man's God-given sexuality and ultimately in total moral depravity.

In Rom 1:18-32, St Paul vividly describes how God *punishes* those who, through pride, reject Him and turn to idols of their own creation. First He makes them spiritually blind and hence prone to a perverted sexuality, clearly delineated as homosexuality and lesbianism. Then they become "filled with every kind of wickedness" and "without conscience"; *encourage others to sin* as themselves; and thus eventually bring about the corruption of the whole of society.

Now, the whole *raison d'etre* of the feminist movement has been to challenge woman's (and hence, man's) God-given nature and role. Cardinal Ratzinger's belief that "the crisis of morality is closely tied to that of woman and her role"[1] is thus highly significant in the light of Rom 1. It highlights the fact that to-day's moral crisis has evolved from the feminist challenge to creation exactly in the manner described by St Paul.

First, feminists rejected the revealed truth of Scripture and Tradition. Tradition was declared to be a "series of human choices" which could be "revoked", and Scripture a

61

collection of myths justifying "patriarchal oppression" that could be re-written from a feminist perspective.[2] Christianity was dismissed as a religion founded by men, a product of a culture that was unfavourable towards women;[3] in fact, asserts Merlin Stone in *When God Was a Woman*, it is a product of *politics*.[4] Stone's speculative conclusions, similar to earlier "romantic" Germanic anthropological theories,[5] are drawn from mythology and admittedly limited data; yet they are presented as "proof" of an ancient conspiracy that used religion to establish and maintain male supremacy.[6] Stone's theories justify the feminist rejection of Christianity and its moral code, and so it is important to look closely at them.

According to Stone (and arch-feminist Rosemary Radford Ruether), the original creator of the universe was the goddess Isis who had various names – such as Gaia (Mother Earth) – in various cultures.[7] The original religion was set up to worship the *Goddess*, the Creatress of Life, the Queen of Heaven, the Mother of God the Father.[8] Pagan male deities were not as important as the Goddess, the principal deity, and were usually just her consorts.[9]

For feminists, goddess-worshipping societies are an important model, as in them women seemingly were community leaders who owned businesses and property. Society was "matrilineal", i.e., children were named after their mothers and inheritance was through the female line; further, women, not men, held the rights to the throne. Most importantly, women were "sexually autonomous", having total sexual freedom.[10]

The female deity was the "patroness of sexual pleasure". Sex, "her gift to humanity", was "sacred and holy" and temples were houses of prostitution in her honour.[11] The unmarried mother was "worshipped", her children were legitimate, adultery was "glorified", and divorce and abortions were easily obtained.[12] "Kings" were merely sexual partners of the high priestess, who was also queen, and were regularly replaced through ritual sacrifice.[13]

This female paradise, stretching from the Mediterranean to India, supposedly started disappearing with the invasions of the Indo-Europeans. The invaders worshipped a supreme male (pagan) deity, having at some stage "abandoned" matriarchy. Stone assumes that they presented their male deities as superior to the female deities of the conquered lands, and in order to justify male supremacy, taught that the universe was created by a male god who instituted kingship. The Indo-Aryans did not try to destroy the sexual customs of the conquered nations, but their "patriarchal" religion, family system and form of government gradually reduced the economic and sexual status of women.[14]

It was the later-invading Hebrews who attempted to destroy the Goddess religion. They supposedly obtained not only their account of creation, but also their ideas of "male supremacy", patrilineal descent and permanent kingship from the Indo-Europeans. But the sexual customs of the Goddess-worshipping nations prevented knowledge of the *paternity* of children, necessary for a patrilineal system of inheritance. So, in order to obtain land and governmental control, i.e., political power, the Levite priests denounced these customs and "devised the concept of sexual 'morality': premarital virginity (and) marital fidelity for *women*" which gave them "total control over knowledge of paternity".[15]

Christianity continued with a "more extreme suppression" of the Goddess religion for the same reasons. In order to "maintain a male-dominated society", it "adopted" the Hebrew "myth" of Adam and Eve which "justified male ownership and control of women" as being the divine will.[16] The politically-devised tenets of Judeo-Christian theologies and their "patriarchal" attitudes towards the differing roles of men and women then became "so deeply ingrained" that they *came to be* considered natural tendencies and were absorbed into secular life and social customs, thus finally

63

destroying "the female religions, female sexual autonomy and matrilineal descent".[17]

The convoluted logic used in rationalizing the rejection of revelation, natural law, Judaism and Christianity is symptomatic of the loss of faith. Spiritual blindness and the loss of morals follow logically (and as predicted by St Paul). After all, if Christianity is a religion devised by scheming men, then the Decalogue can – indeed, *should* – be rejected. Christian sexual ethics, in particular, are only tools for men to control women's bodies; so the fundamental approach of the women's liberation movement has been to remove this control.[18] The suppression of women's rites is seen as the suppression of women's rights to "reproductive self-determination, sex education, birth control, abortion and lesbianism", rights to sexual autonomy which "for thousands of years helped women to retain their independence economically, socially and legally".[19]

But the rejection of Christian morality by a tiny minority of Christians could not by itself produce a *social order* in which women could live as "mature, self-determining human beings".[20] Nineteenth-century feminists tried to initiate a return to goddess worship and paganism, but they were unsuccessful.[21] It was only after feminism allied itself with Marxism that it was able to bring about changes in civil laws that were preventing the sexual autonomy of women and its attendant economic benefits.[22]

Since many turn-of-the-century feminists equated Socialism with social progress, after the theory of a universal primitive matriarchal civilization was "absorbed" into Socialism by Engels, it became "a standard part of Socialist social history" for feminist Socialists. They saw primitive matriarchy as the "original stage of communal society where woman('s) . . . labor and sexuality was (sic) at her own disposal. Patriarchy came about through the rise of private property" and the desire for a patrilineal system of inheritance. It "resulted in the subjugation of women", so feminists had "to advance to the Socialist revolution"; for besides ideological support, Communism provided them with a working example of a society in which women had full and equal employment with men, i.e., economic independence, which "was seen as the key to women's liberation".[23]

Now, Communism is a tool of Freemasonry, as Marx and Engels were commissioned by the Illuminati to write the *Communist Manifesto* which professes Illuminati ideology.[24] Masonry works to corrupt mankind by "making enviable the state of the savage" whose happiness was destroyed by religion. It finds the corruption of women in particular essential for the destruction of its main target: Catholicism.[25] The concept of equality of the sexes, which has seduced feminists, can be recognized as an offshoot of the Masonic (and Communist) doctrine of absolute equality that involves the suppression of all distinctions and makes necessary the destruction of hierarchy and family life.[26]

Communism has made this goal practical by its "rejection of any link that binds woman to the family and home", and its proclamation of her emancipation as "a basic principle".[27] Wishing to "restore women to economic autonomy", the "main socialist agenda has been to integrate women into the work force", making them "independent wage earners" and "equal partners" with men "on the job and within marriage". This has necessitated state-supported day-care centres; maternity leave with guaranteed re-entry to jobs; low-cost or free contraceptives and abortions; and the "dismantling" of "patriarchal laws that discriminated againt women in marriage and divorce".[28] These provisions of the Communist state are precisely the civil "rights" that feminists have been fighting for – and have largely won – in what was once Christendom.

The Church teaches that men and women are equal in dignity as persons created in the image of God and as children of God called to union with Him in eternal life. The indissolubility of the marriage bond safeguards the equality of the spouses and the dignity of woman. But the equality of spouses is limited, first "by the distinctive qualities which nature has bestowed on each sex", and which "nothing short of wilful blindness, or a doctrinaire attitude as disastrous as it is utopian, can ignore", and second, by the "necessary hierarchy in the society of the family".[29] Hence, affirmed Pope Pius XII, "the present structure of society, based on the almost absolute equality of man and woman, rests on a false presumption".[30]

As seen, this presumption, adopted in order to effect women's economic liberation, has entailed the rejection of the God-given roles for men and women inscribed in the laws of nature and the rupture of the "indissoluble bond between sexuality and motherhood".[31] But, since "the language of nature is also the language of morality",[32] women's rejection of the natural law for atheistic, pagan ideals of womanhood is having the predicted devastating effects on civilization.

It has led to procreation without sexuality (e.g. *in vitro* fertilization and surrogate motherhood) and the idea that every form of sexuality is equivalent; so we have the tragic situation of a chastisement of God (Rom 1:26-28) actually inscribed as a "right" in human laws that sanction homosexuality and extend to homosexual "marriages" with social benefits given to families. Pleasure is the only point of sex and life, and since children hinder the pursuit of pleasure, abortion is institutionalized.[33] Pre-marital cohabitation, adultery, divorce, the retention of her maiden name by a wife and the passing on of it to her children, are quickly completing the conversion of the Christian social structure to that of the matrilineal goddess-worshipping societies.

As if confirming this conversion, the goddess was "resurrected" in a gathering held in her honour in a Boston church in 1976. The connection between moral degeneration and goddess worship was starkly symbolized by bare-breasted women chanting, "The Goddess is alive – Magic (witchcraft) is afoot". They were "proclaiming that being female is divine" as "in feminist witchcraft each woman is a Goddess".[34] Idolatry (the worship of themselves or of Gaia/Isis by feminists) and witchcraft[35] are sins of the flesh (Gal 5:19-20) that, together with sexual perversion, are the end results of feminism because they are the divine chastisements reserved for those who reject God and His plan of creation (Rom 1:18-28).

In spite of Masonic aspirations, the Isis mentality can never destroy the Church as her perpetuity is guaranteed (Mt 16:18); but because it attacks the religious and moral foundations of the family, the basic unit of society,[36] it has "condemned" civilization to "sterility and decline".[37] Pope Pius XII has declared that the solution to the crisis is to form "the Christian women of profound faith and sound morals in every strata of society" using the means of prayer and "absolute faithfulness to the directives" of the Magisterium.[38]

Only God can give "true solutions to the infinitely delicate problems that relate to the role of women" – but He manifests Himself only to the humble and obedient. Mary is our supreme model in humility and obedience, and it is she who can direct the efforts to restore moral and religious integrity and a sense of true values.[39] Exclaimed Pope Pius:

If life reveals to what depths of vice and degradation woman can at times descend, Mary (whose dignity as Mother of God called down upon her extraordinary privileges), shows to what heights she can climb, in and through Christ, even to ascending above all other creatures. What civilization, what religion has ever raised to such heights the ideal of womanhood, or exalted it to such perfection? Modern humanism, laicism, Marxist propaganda . . . non-Christian cults, have nothing to offer which can even be compared with this vision . . . so glorious and so humble, transcendent and (yet) so easily accessible.[40]

The modern cult of Isis owes its success to Communism. Our Lady of Fatima promised that if we follow her directives, she will bring to an end the errors of Russia. "Communism is dead"! cries a blinded world that proclaimed "God is dead"! a while ago. The latter sentiment is not true; we can consider the former true when feminism and feminist-generated corruption collapse, and the Immaculate Heart of Mary reigns triumphant over a world restored to purity and obedience to the will of its Creator.[41]

REFERENCES

1. Joseph Ratzinger with Vittorio Messori, *The Ratzinger Report,* trans. Salvator Attanasio and Graham Harrison, San Francisco, Ignatius Press, 1985, p 93.
2. Cornelia R Ferreira, "The Feminist Agenda Within the Church", *Homiletic & Pastoral Review,* May 1987, p 12, or pamphlet, *The Feminist Agenda Within the Catholic Church,* Toronto, Life Ethics Centre, 1987, pp 4-5; *idem.,* "The Emerging Feminist Religion", *Homiletic & Pastoral Review,* May 1989 pp 15-16, or pamphlet, *The Emerging Feminist Religion,* Toronto, Life Ethics Centre, 1989, p 6.
3. *Declaration on the Admission of Women to the Ministerial Priesthood, Inter Insigniores,* 1974, 4.
4. Merlin Stone, *When God Was a Woman,* New York, Harcout, Brace, Jovanovich, 1978, pp xxvi, 166, 66, 131.
5. Rosemary Radford Ruether, as cited in Cornelia R Ferreira, "The Destructive Forces Behind Religious Feminism", in *Feminism v. Mankind,* ed. Christine M Kelly, Wicken, Milton Keynes, UK, Family Publications, 1990, p 54; Stone, p 33.
6. Stone, pp xxv, 66-67, 33, 156, 240-41.
7. *Ibid.,* pp xxv, 219, xx, 9, 2-4, 89-90, 22-23; Rosemary Radford Ruether, *Sexism and God-Talk: Toward a Feminist Theology,* Boston, Beacon Press, 1983, pp 1-3.
8. Stone, p 1,9; Ruether, p 2.
9. Stone, pp 26-29, 96, 99-100, 134, 137, 164-165.
10. *Ibid.,* pp 157, 11-12, 31-32, 45-47, 129, 182.
11. *Ibid.,* pp 154-155, 217. Note that Stone takes great exception to the use of the words "prostitute" for the "sanctified women" of the temple or "prostitution" for the "sacred sexual customs of the female religion", pp 157, xx.
12. *Ibid.,* pp 159, 43, 53-54, 59, 131-32.
13. *Ibid.,* pp 96-97, 131-139, 151.
14. *Ibid.,* pp 61, 66-67, 69, 156.
15. *Ibid.,* pp 68-69, 108-111, 166, 189-190, 156, 161-162, 179, 217-219.
16. *Ibid.,* pp 193-94, 218-24, 68-69, 162.
17. *Ibid.,* pp xxvi, 239-240, 228, 68.
18. Ruether, p 228 (note that Ruether defines patriarchy as "the subordination of women's bodies, sexuality and reproduction to male ownership and control").
19. Stone, pp 228, 179; Ruether, p 217.
20. *Ibid.,* p xxvi

21. Ferreira, "Destructive Forces", pp 53, 55, 59. 22. Ruether, pp 221, 221-222, 104; Fereira, pp 58-59.
23. Rosemary Radford Ruether, "Radical Victorians: The Quest for an Alternative Culture", *Women and Religion in America*, vol 3, 1900-1968, ed. Rosemary Radford Ruether and Rosemary Skinner Keller, San Francisco, Harper and Row, 1986, pp 4-5; *idem., Sexism and God-Talk*, p 224.
24. Deirdre Manifold, *Karl Marx: True or False Prophet?*, Galway, Firenne Publications, 1985, pp 72, 76, 78-79.
25. Jose Maria Cardinal Caro y Rodriguez, *The Mystery of Freemasonry Unveiled*, Santiago, Society of the Good Press, reprint ed. Hawthorne, CA: Christian Book Club of America, 1971, pp 234-237.
26. *Ibid.*, pp 42-43, Pope Pius XI, encyclical letter *On Atheistic Communism*, 19 March 1937, 10.
27. Pope Pius XI, *ibid.*, ll.
28. Ruether, *Sexism and God-Talk*, pp 223-224. Note that secular humanism, which has also aided the feminist cause, is allied with Marxism: Ferreira, *ibid.*, pp 57-59.
29. Popes Leo XIII, Pius XI and Pius XII, as cited in *The Woman in the Modern World*, ed. the Monks of Solesmes, Boston, The Daughters of St Paul, 1959, pp 35-37, 66-67, 90-91, 128-129 and Analytical Index, pp 22-23.
30. *Ibid.*, p 109.
31. Cardinal Ratzinger, p 84.
32. *Ibid.*, p 97.
33. Cf., *ibid.*, pp 84-86.
34. Naomi R Goldenberg, *Changing of the Gods: Feminism and the End of Traditional Religions*, Boston, Beacon Press, 1979, pp 92-93.
35. Ferreira, "Feminist Agenda", pp 14-16 (pamphlet, pp 8-12). Witchcraft is inextricably linked with goddess worship as it is the only means for expressing this idolatry. Feminism today fits right in with the occult Gaia (Mother Earth) – worshipping New Age Movement: Catherine Dunphy, "Return of the Goddess", *Toronto Star*, 30 June,1990, p J1.
36. Second Vatican Ecumenical Council, Decree on the Apostolate of the Laity *Apostolicam Actuositatem*, 1965, 11.
37. Pope Pius XII cited in *The Woman in the Modern World*, pp 112, 302.
38. Pope Pius XII, *ibid.*, p 224.
39. *Ibid.*, p 252.
40. *Ibid.*, p 305.
41. St Maximilian Kolbe taught that the title of "Immaculate" refers not only to Mary's absolute purity, but also to her perfect obedience. He founded the still extant movement *Militia Immaculatae* under the inspiration of Our Lady in order to fight the Freemasons and other agents of Lucifer by fostering in minds and hearts a sharing in her perfect obedience. Bernard M Geiger, OFM Conv., *Kolbe's "Blueprint" for World Unity*, Libertyville, Il., Prow Books/Franciscan Marytown Press, 1972, pp 9, 12-15, 20-21.

Five:

The fruit of their doings

Feminism, Priesthood and the Anglican Communion

Dori Watson Boynton

Is the priesting of women a shining achievement of the "social justice movement" as some believe? Is it at the same time the principle tactic in the dark war being waged against Christendom? Is it perhaps the primary impetus behind what Graham Leonard, Anglican Bishop of London, calls the "re-alignment of Christendom"? Is it, then, God's means for cleansing His Holy Church?

This essay will examine some feminist aims and attitudes and the related experience of the Episcopal Church (the small but influential American province of the Anglican Communion). Here, the anomalous "priesting" of women has gone on for some fifteen years, and more than a thousand women have been "ordained". In those years, additional points in the feminist agenda have become clear and are being implemented.

"Feminist vision is a new movement for our time . . . (it) leaves few issues unaddressed . . . Feminist vision is not progressive or liberal; it is radical and revolutionary. The Christian Church has yet to know what kind of impact the preaching of feminist vision will have on its own life and the life and structures of our larger society and world".[1] This is feminist rhetoric. It should be taken seriously. Feminists have succeeded in being priested even though women "priests" are inimical to Holy Orders and where women "priests" are found, the icon of the sacred priesthood is shattered. Further, their presence assures that feminist aims will supersede Christian principles as has been demonstrated in a Church that has become increasingly enshrouded in "the atmosphere of a thickening apostasy".[2] The same revolution is occurring throughout Christendom, so what is recounted here is a cautionary tale.

One of the earliest clear articulations of the feminist religious view was written by Mary Daly, some twenty years ago:

> The new wave of feminism desperately needs to be not only many-faceted but cosmic and ultimately religious in vision. This means reaching outward and inward toward the God beyond and beneath the gods who have stolen our identity . . . As the essential victims of the archaic God projections, women can bring this process of creativity into a new phase. This involves iconoclasm, the breaking of idols. The basic idol breaking will be done on the level of internalized images of male superiority, on the plane of exorcising them from consciousness and from the cultural institutions that breed them.[3]

(Note: Daly's "idol" is the traditional Christian's sacred symbol and icon).

In two respects, the present iconoclasm differs from the Eighth Century heresy. Then, iconoclasts "broke" only the holy pictures and they left a devotional vacuum; present iconoclasts are deliberately breaking all Christian symbols and icons and simultaneously re-filling them with a new syncretistic religion. In the words of one woman:

> Symbol systems cannot simply be rejected, they must be replaced. Where there is not any replacement, the mind will revert to familiar structures at times of crisis, bafflement or defeat.[4]

The new iconoclasm, though a product of feminism, is but another face of modernism which the Enclyclical *Pascendi*

Gregis described as "the synthesis of all heresies".[5] Many seasons of the covert agnosticism of Biblical Higher Criticism prepared the way for the overt modernism that has swept the Episcopal Church for three decades. From this agnostic basis (described in detail in the Encyclical, see note 5) which permeated Anglican ivory towers, the deconstruction of the Episcopal Church took three outward forms, the first being pivotal. First, General Convention, once only the *governing* body of the Episcopal Church, arrogated to itself the authority to *change Christian doctrine* (in the 1960s, but most dramatically from the 1976 Minneapolis Convention onwards; the ordination of women was the issue). Second was the "priesting" of women itself, and third was the replacement of the 1928 *Book of Common Prayer* which provided a standard for faith and practice. The first not only made the second two (and any subsequent) changes possible, it literally changed the nature of the Church from being doctrinally Christian to a humanist institution. That is, man's dispensations replaced Christian revelation; the institutional Church had placed itself in schism from the One Holy Catholic Church which is God's.

In those tumultuous years roughly a third of the members left the Church. Those remaining comprise three groups: the people enthusiastic for the "revolutionary" changes; those (principally members of the Episcopal Synod whose director stated recently, "the Church's present crisis . . . will be resolved only when the Church returns to her doctrinal and liturgical moorings"[6]) who resist the modernist innovations; and those who identify "Church" principally as ecclesiastical edifices and/or a corporate institution, and are just staying put.

George MacDonald, C S Lewis' mentor, observed:

> I doubt if any man can ever be sure that a thing is the will of God, save by seeing into its nature and character, and beholding its goodness.[7]

And as C S Lewis himself asked, so one must also ask of

whatever modernist one may encounter, that

> . . . the skeptical element in your mind . . . not be reserved exclusively for the New Testament and the Creeds. Try doubting something else.[8]

(That the priesting of women is God's will, for example).

Dr Robert M Strippy, former staff member of the ECUSA Executive Council and one time director of research for *The Episcopalian,* pointed out even before the 1976 Convention that the liberal movement (as he says, the older name for it is modernism)

> . . . is out to destroy the traditional basis of authority and also the sacraments. That is to say, in the church they visualise they will use the *form* of the sacrament, but they are utterly unwilling to accept their *substance.* They do not believe in the sacraments. They do not regard them as a means of grace, but merely as symbols of God's love . . . It is this anti-sacramental bent − and not any concern for women's rights − that is behind the liberals' push for women's ordination.[9]

In the Episcopal Church, the 1976 General Convention vote on women's ordination was forced by the renegade "ordination" on 29 July 1974, of eleven women in Philadelphia. Three retired bishops (Corrigan, DeWitt and Welles), setting aside the scriptural faith and tradition they were bound to uphold, asserted their "belief that the Church was violating God's will in barring women from the priesthood . . . "[10] The Board of Inquiry Majority report goes on to explain that the bishops

> . . . offer this belief as a justification for their conduct on July 29, 1974. While the four bishops undoubtedly believe that the ordinations are valid, their extraordinary action was in a sense symbolic, designed at least in part to teach and to urge change to comply with their view of 'true' doctrine.[11]

Just prior to the event, Bishop DeWitt told Bishop Paul Moore, Jr (Diocese of New York), "We have been meeting with some of the women and I think the only way is to just do it."[12] Reportedly this upset Moore, because they were violating

> an ancient law and custom of the Church . . . (and also) were about to dishonour the administrative rules as well. Contrary to what those rules required, none of the eleven women had been approved for ordination by their own bishops and standing committees; nor had DeWitt, Corrigan and Welles received permission from the Bishop of Pennsylvania to conduct ordinations in his diocese. So the ordinations would be illegal and irregular on every conceivable ground.[13]

It was this embarrassment that bothered Moore. He himself was, in fact, one of the several liberal bishops who

> . . . had decided the time had come to press for the ordination of women into the priesthood, for a change in the apostolic tradition . . . But he thought he and his colleagues had agreed that the breakthrough should be made legally, that *they should agitate within the highest councils of the Church.*[14]

(Emphasis added. The tendency of such Episcopal Bishops to identify "the Church" with the *Episcopal* Church displays a remarkable hubris. It also, as in this instance, begs the central question of the debate.)

The "Philadelphia eleven"[15] and the "maverick" bishops produced "a ministry of division and antagonism", as a Canon, then living in Oxford termed it. In an open letter from England to the participating bishops, he went on to ask:

> How can I receive communion from the hands of those whose ministry has been given to them not for the purpose of maintaining community but of fomenting disunity, a ministry which does not have for its purpose the building

up of the body but of tearing it apart, a ministry which, in the literal meaning of the words, is not sym-bolic (throwing together) but dia-bolic (throwing apart)?[16]

The question was prophetic; it continues to be asked. The Canon also remarked:

It seems that you have used these women as a tool for turning your private beliefs into a public battle.[17]

In this he was only half right: the women had an agenda of their own and could have been similarly charged.
Peter Mills noted:

In her autobiography, *Womanpriest*, the Rev Alla Bozarth-Campbell justified her illegal ordination in 1974 by asserting that most people are converted by the accomplished fact; that is, that anything she wanted but they did not had to be forced upon them.[18]

And the struggle continues as modernist bishops compel priests to accept as doctrine what traditional Christian bishops, priests and laity regard as invalid and heretical.[19]

The means used to bring about canonical "approval" (and hence, doctrinal "authority") for women's ordination were less than candid, and were based on *in camera* word juggling and "democratic" vote.[20] Thus, the Episcopal Church did not choose to have women "priests"; the innovation was thrust on the Church by a small inner ring of modernists. A loud claque then raised the cry, "there is no theological objection to women priests". It has seemed to the traditional Christian that indeed there is every theological objection, but somehow the point was never clarified.[21] Further, those who instigated the novelty declined to spell out their theological rationale *for* priesting women. Recently, however, "certain women theologians" have done so as part of a Response and Resolution to be studied along with the Eames Report[22] and intended for presentation at the 1990 House of Bishops' Meeting. Its purpose was to fault the Eames Commission for foot-dragging and waffling, and to demand "provisionality" be set aside. ("Provisionality" adopts the Gamaliel[23] approach to the question: let's try it for a while and see if God prospers it or lets it wither.)

The women urge the full recognition of women as priests immediately and universally. To back up their demand they spell out their supporting doctrine. It can be summed up in four words. Women can be priests *because they are human*.[24] They say:

> . . . if every human being is, by virtue of being human, fit 'matter' for baptism, every human being is also fit 'matter' for ordination. (Sec II:4)[25]

The "Women Theologians" add:

> By contrast, the arguments brought to bear against the ordination of women are all culturally relative, based on world-views, including that of the first century, that regard women as inherently inferior creatures, less than fully human. (Sec II:8)[26]

Obviously, Christian doctrine is be-fogged and bent. For, as Archbishop Louis Falk of the Anglican Catholic Church has pointed out, it is not the humanity of Christ which is salvific ('humanity' being an abstraction) but the *personhood*, and Jesus the Person in whom were united divinity and humanity, was male. Thus the argument (of Ackland and others) amounts essentially to a heresy with regard to the doctrine of the Incarnation.

What the women offer as Christian theology is neither Christian nor theological, it is full-blown modernism and anti-Christian, "revolutionary" rhetoric. It is, in fact, anti-Doctrine, and reminds us of the words of Pope John Paul II addressed to American Catholics in his 1976 visit to the States:

> We are now facing the final confrontation between the Church and anti-Church, of the Gospel versus the anti-

Gospel. This confrontation lies within the plans of divine Providence; it is a trial the whole Church . . . must take up.[27]

Speaking as a traditional Christian layman, Barbara Rhett counters the modernist/feminist notions with, "No truth of God can become an untruth because of our transitory religous caprices".[28] Further, it must be stated clearly and unequivocally that however pleasant an individual feminist personality may be, feminism from its very inception has been anti-Christian in principle. Its aims are antithetical to traditional Christianity and the Christian Church.[29]

These aims also bear no relationship to the Christian idea in character, attitudes and virtues. Self-pity, envy, contempt, rage and all the other expressions of impotence and thwarted (or "realized", which is worse) self-importance that fuel feminism are at variance with "the mind of Christ Jesus". In the words of one feminist:

> I am struck by the powerful anger (my early essays) express and by the transformative power the expression of my anger at God has had in my life . . . The sisterhood of the woman's movement gave me permission to express my anger at the patriarchal society that had thwarted and crippled me.[30]

The group that controls and governs the Episcopal Church not only seems to have a different agenda but also to be on a completely different "wave length" from traditional Christians. Carter Heyward tells us:

> During the 1970s socialist feminism began to emerge in the United States and Europe as a critique of white western patriarchal culture – in particular, of its idealization of the autonomous white male's right to social and economic power.[31]

Described on her book-jacket as "Episcopal priest and professor of theology at Episcopal Divinity School in

Cambridge, Massachusetts", Mrs Heyward describes herself thus:

> I am a white anglo southern christian (sic) lesbian priest and academic with class roots in middle-strata United States of America. I am teacher and learner, activist and theorist, well educated by life as well as by school in classical feminist western culture. I am interested in multi-cultural and global realities, and hope someday to better understand them.[32]

From such seminaries and modernist/feminist revolutionaries issues the siren call which

> . . . dwells on the introduction of a new order of Christian life, on new directions of the Church, on new aspirations of the modern soul, on a new social vocation of the clergy, on a new Christian civilization, and many other things of the same kind.[33]

Whether religious feminists remain associated with ecclesiastical structures or disassociate themselves from them, their religious "world-view" is basically the same (though it serves a tactical purpose, the anti-Christian bent is disguised). Similarly, their views are shared or have been adopted as useful by other modernists (liberals). For feminists do have what all the modernists need: a religious world-view to replace the Christian content as the Christian icons are shattered. In their hands, the icons and symbols are used to contain a syncretized amalgam (of pantheism, subjectivism, relativism, humanism, scientism, Marxism, materialism, pansexualism, etc.)

The more of the feminist/modernist writings one reads, the more uniform they sound. But after all, their authors are all revolutionaries with a common cause. As one prominent modernist Episcopalian Bishop himself tells us:

> I am convinced that the church conservatives have understood and appreciated more profoundly the

dimensions of this revolution that have the church liberals. The liberals tend to see the woman's movement, for example, primarily in terms of justice and human rights. That is too shallow a judgement in my view. The conservatives, on the other hand, see the woman's movement as a fundamental break with history and tradition . . . They recognize, as the liberals seem not to do, that much of what we Christians think of as crucial to the life of the church will not survive the revolution . . . They are correct.[34]

The shattering of the icon of the priesthood has been accomplished canonically and physically in the Episcopal Church. (That is, at the official institutional level as well as implemented by placement of hundreds of women "priests" in parishes, seminaries, chaplaincies, etc.). With this success, further icons of the faith could then systematically and openly be placed under attack. Thus, more of the feminist package is revealed and one is given a clearer picture of what is in store for a successfully "revolutionized" Church. The feminist rationale for the revolution rests on a patently skewed view of the Church. Mary Daly, for example, argues that the core symbolism of Christianity communicates "that maleness is divine".[35] According to Daly

. . . the image of the Father God spawned in the human imagination and sustained . . . by patriarchy (produces a context in which) mystification of roles takes place: the husband dominating his wife represents God himself.[36]

Such rhetoric is demagoguery, which, as Marxist Antonio Gramschi explains, is "a general set of mind by which, in order to vanquish one's adversary, one neglects considerations that might support his position".[37]

On such questionable grounds stands the feminist demand for inclusive language "What we (are) talking about is 'people language' not 'God language'",[38] for "gender-free" liturgies, and for the revision of Holy Scripture according to feminist guidelines. The inclusive language demand is absurd in the Christian view. As one-time editor of *The Living Church,* Dr Carroll Simcox pointed out:

> To discontinue calling humanity 'man' out of respect for our mothers and sisters and wives is in effect to exclude them from the human race.[39]

Thus in the second "inclusive language" rite for the Holy Eucharist now being tested, the Creation texts are revised to present a feminine image of God:

> Your spirit moved over the deep and brought to birth the heavens: sun, moon and stars; earth, winds, and waters; growing plants and animals; and finally humankind.[40]

Giving birth to creation replaces God the Creator with "Mother"/Goddess; this

> . . . is the view that God and the cosmos are ultimately identical. That is a good definition of both secularism and paganism.[41]

What Gramschi described as "the will to liberation" is an interconnecting or encompassing will. In one brief paragraph in a modernist, homosexual priest's autobiography one reads:

> The goal is the creation of a *new person.* It is not a matter of "struggling for others", which suggests paternalism and reformist objectives, but rather of becoming aware of oneself as not completely fulfilled and as living in an alienated society, according to Gustave Gutierrez in *A Theology of Liberation.* The denial of one's sexual rights, indeed sexual identity, stands in the way of 'complete fulfilment' and surely bars an experience of 'solidarity with all humankind'.[42]

The erasure of gender distinctions and the pan-sexuality that upholds the commission of homosexual acts are tied to "justice" in the modernist view. As Carter Heyward says in *Touching Our Strength:*

I am reflecting on the erotic as our embodied yearning for maturity. As such, I am interested not merely in a 'theology of sexuality' – examining sexuality through theological lenses; but rather in probing the Sacred – exploring the divine terrain – through sexual experience. In these pages with Audre Lorde, I want 'to write fire' to be erotic – touching, pressing, making connections, contributing what I can to the forging of that mutuality which characterizes right relation or justice.[43]

It is in the context of this re-definition of "justice" that the priesting of women is demanded. Modernists accomplish much because they use traditional Christian terminology to present concepts which are the exact opposite of what that terminology once expressed. As Archbishop Falk has said:

At least at the time of the French Revolution the Devil had the honesty to have his adherents admit openly that they were proffering a completely new religion with completely new terminology. I suspect he learnt something from that failure.

So un-Christian and anti-Christian ideas and innovations are "sold" to trustful Christians, and a Christian Church is de-Christianized. There is a pattern to all this, and it is what Dr Joseph Farrell and B W Anderson refer to as "the pattern of apostasy". In the clearest possible (indeed the most literal) instance of apostasy's underlying principle (which, according to Farrell and Anderson is to "disguise unbelief; put virtue in the service of vice",[44] Bishop Paul Moore, Jr in January 1977 "ordained" avowed and practising lesbian Ellen Barrett, because of her "honesty".[45]

In the picture as a whole, only one thing is certain; Christian practice and standards have been replaced by situational arbitrariness. The positions of two seminaries may be mentioned to illustrate this. Both are modern and feminist in that they advocate and train women "priests". In the 1990 theological journal of one is a long article which argues the moral neutrality of homosexual acts and claims to offer "a more reasonable approach" to "gay men and lesbians and their holy unions".[46] The 1990 theological journal of the other states an opposite position, disapproving "of sexual intercourse outside the bonds of marriage, adulterous relationships, and the practice of homosexuality".[47] Such variety does not signal, as it once did, the tolerance that has long been a hallmark of Anglicanism, but rather, that the revolution is still in process. The Church has been liberated from the traditional Christian priesthood; it has yet to be liberated completely from traditional Christian morality.

Meanwhile, what of individual souls? For that, after all, is what a Christian church is all about. A resolution was placed before the 1990 Convention of the Diocese of Pennsylvania:

> Resolved: that we "do believe the Holy Scriptures of the Old and New Testaments to be the Word of God and to contain all things necessary to salvation", and we do believe, in accordance with the same Scripture and our Anglican tradition, that "Jesus is the Christ, the only name under heaven by which we may be saved".

The resolution was defeated. Apparently, as Fr David Ousley oberved, "a majority do not accept and obey a religion revealed by God".[48] If the two or three gathered together are non-believers, the icon of Church as the faithful gathered together is surely shattered. Equally surely, countless souls are in jeopardy.

So one Christian ponders:

> As I reflected back upon my own parish's stormy history . . . I realized that, along with the weekly Holy Communion (which we had then, because 20 years ago we had three services on Sunday), we now have a great deal of liturgical pagentry and much 'togetherness' – hugging, kissing, dancing, talking – any time, any place. In many ways, the service has lost much sense of the transcendent

in this progressive 'revolution'.

Moreover, once upon a time I could expect to find the Eucharist on BCP (Book of Common Prayer) feast days and holy days – now they have disappeared from our parish's weekly calendar, and share Sunday with whatever else is on the agenda – in October Youth Sunday, Aids Sunday and Alcohol Awareness Sunday. We have lost any sense of communion with those who for centuries celebrated on a particular day, however inconvenient it was. Unfortunately, it reminds me of a group of witty essays by Dorothy L Sayers called the *Pantheon Paper*, in which she described her contemporary church as using a Polar Year for its calendar, during which it celebrated such seasons as Advertisement Trash Wednesday and Civilization Sunday.[49]

To his own time and, apparently increasingly, to ours the prophet Micah cries:

. . . the land shall be desolate because of them that dwell therein, for the fruit of their doings. (7:13)

But the Church is God's, not man's and Christianity is still on the loose, "Because", as a Christian poet affirms so truly:

. . . the Holy Ghost over the bent world broods with warm breast and ah! bright wings.

REFERENCES

1. Christine M Smith, *Weaving the Sermon: Preaching in a Feminist Perspective*, Louisville, Kentucky, Westminster/John Knox Press, 1989, p 104.
2. Constantine, Archimandrite of Jordanville, "Before the Face of Antichrist", Appendix II, in Archbishop Averky, *Apocalypse*, trans. Fr Seraphim Rose, Platina, California, St Hermes of Alaska Brotherhood, 1985, p 232.
3. Mary Daly, "Why Speak About God?", *Womanspirit Rising: A Feminist Reader in Religion*, ed. C Christ and J Plaskow, New York, Harper and Row, 1979, p 211.
4. Carol P. Christ, "Why Women Need the Goddess", *ibid.*, p 275.
5. Pope Pius X, Encyclical *Pascendi Gregis*, Official translation, London, Burns and Oates, Long Prairie, Minnesota, The Newman Press, 1983, Passim.

6. J.F. Titus Oates, "Traditionalists Pointing Toward General Convention", *Foundations*, I, No 9, November, 1990, (Fort Worth, Texas), p 1.
7. George MacDonald, *Robert Falconer*, Eureka, California, Sunrise Books, 1990, p 101.
8. C S Lewis, "Modern Theology and Biblical Criticism", *Christian Reflections*, ed. Walter Hooper, Grand Rapids, William B Eerdmans, 1985, p 164.
9. Robert C. Harvey, *A House Divided*, Dumont, New Jersey, The Canterbury Guild, 1976, pp 49-50.
10. Board of Inquiry, "Certificate of Determination and Majority Report", New York, Office of the Presiding Bishop of the Episcopal Church, March 26, 1975, p 3.
11. *Ibid.*
12. Jervis Anderson, "Standing Out There On The Issues: Bishop Paul Moore, Jr", *The New Yorker*, 28 April 1986, p 88.
13. *Ibid.*
14. *Ibid.*
15. Jeanette Piccard, Sr Alla Bozarth-Campbell, Betty Bone Schiess, Alison Cheek, Merrill Bittner, Nancy Wittig, Suzanne Hiatt, Katrina Swanson, Maria Moorefield, Carter Heyward and Emily Hewitt.
16. John H. Heidt, Open letter quoted in "The Philadelphia Ordinations", *The Living Church*, 1 September 1974, p 7.
17. *Ibid.*
18. David Peter Mills, "The Evangelical Catholic", quoted in *The American Church Digest of the Traditional Christian Voice*, prepared for the 1988 Lambeth Conference, Greenwich, Connecticut, Internation Council for the Apostolic Faith, 1988, p 24.
19. Bishop H Coleman McGehee, Jr, The Episcopal Diocese of Michigan, Pastoral letter signed by H Coleman McGehee Jr (Diocesan Bishop), R Steward Wood Jr (Bishop Coadjutor) and H Irving Mayson (Bishop Syffragan), computer printout from Ronald Ring, Attorney, 27 Nov 1989, 09:55, p 1.

Note: One recent example is a modernist bishop's pastoral letter issued by an attorney's office ordering the priests in the diocese to recognize "the validity of the order of our female colleagues" because "the ordination of women in the Episcopal Church is established doctrine". He adds, "Our communion's heritage certainly allows room for those who regret this turn of events but does not licence behaviour degrading to an entire sex. Women waited patiently over the centuries, accepting the sacrament from the hands of even the most demented misogynists, while being denied not only ordination, but even membership in the governing bodies of the Church; and they did so without threatening the unity of the Church . . Tolerance, openness and diversity are cornerstones of our tradition and corporate life. However, even in such a tradition and corporate life certain *behavior* cannot be condoned, and that includes disrespect for any person and the negation of that persons ordination.

20. The process is described by William Stringfellow and Anthony Towne in Part Two, "The Ordination of Women", *The Death and Life of Bishop Pike*, New York, Doubleday, 1976, pp 315-319.

Note: The "revision" of Christian doctrine by the manipulation of canonical language went something like this: let us say that those of the lay order of deaconesses were not "appointed" but "ordered" (agreed); if "ordered", then they constitute a fourth "order" (agreed); if they are a fourth order, it must be Order (i.e. of Holy Order) (agreed): if they constitute an Order, since there isn't any such thing as a fourth "order", it must actually be the third Order (agreed): thus, deaconesses must actually be deacons (agreed); and if they already *are* deacons, there is no reason women cannot be priests and bishops as well. (The bishops that assented to the construction of this heresy automatically place themselves in schism; to function sacramentally with them likewise places other bishops in schism. That is, they separate themselves by advocating something that is at variance with or offers an alternative to traditional Christian doctrine which is encompassed by the Vincentian formula: "(That faith is catholic) which has been believed always, everywhere, and by all". *Commonitorium*, ch 2).

21. Richard A Norris, Jr, Eugene R Fairweather, J E Griffiss and Albert T Mollegen, "A Report on the Validity of the Philadelphia Ordinations", Rochester, Office of the Bishop, Diocese of Rochester, January 30, 1975, Passim.

Note: There were countless discussions, but probably the only clear theological statement was sent by Robert R Spears, Jr, Bishop of Rochester to "the Bishops of the Church" in January, 1975. It was written by four theologians, was not for general distribution, but rather served to set out the Church's official (i.e. liberal/modernist) theological position which, in the spirit of collegiality, the bishops were expected to support. (That is, it spelled out the ideological argument for women's ordination). This document offered the same modernist theology as that of "certain Women Theologians" (see ref.24) E

22. For an analysis of the modernism of the Eames Report and Conclusion, see Dori Watson Boynton, "The Lord's Controversy", Parts I and II, *The Rock*, VII, No 4, December 1989 and VIII, No 3, September 1990, Ladysmith, BC, Canada.

Note: The Eames Report ("Report of the Archbishop of Canterbury's Commission on Communion and Women in the Episcopate") was produced in 1989 by a committee chaired by Archbishop Eames, Anglican Primate of the Church of Ireland and was intended to address the question of how to remain a Communion (or, remain *in* communion) as women were made "bishops" (or "femishops", in Barbara Rhett's lexicon), an anomaly traditional Christians cannot accept. The Report bypassed the essential, fundamental question of whether women can be deacons and priests.

23. Acts 5:34-39.
24. Lauren Ackland, Angela Askew, Vesta Kowalski, Linda Stronhmier and Patricia Wilson-Kastner, "A Theological Response to *The Archbishops' and Primates' Report*" for presentation as a Resolution, Meeting of the House of Bishops, September, 1990.
25. *Ibid.*
26. *Ibid.*
27. John Paul II, as quoted in Randy England, *Unicorn in the Sanctuary: The Impact of the New Age on the Catholic Church*, Manassas, Virginia, Trinity Communications, 1990, p 155.
28. Barbara Cornell Rhett, "Situation Hopeless? No, it is Not!", *The Seabury Journal*, II, No 4, September 1984, Fairfield, Connecticut, p 18.
29. See Cornelia R Ferreira, "The Destructive Forces Behind Religious Feminism", *Feminism v. Mankind*, Wicken, Milton Keynes, Family Publications, 1990, pp 53-60.
30. Carol P Christ, *Laughter of Aphrodite: Reflections on a Journey to the Goddess*, New York, Harper and Row, 1987, p 11.
31. Carter Heywood, *Touching Our Strength: The Erotic as Power and the Love of God*, New York, Harper and Row, 1989, p 16.
32. *Ibid.* p 8.
33. Pope Leo XIII, quoted in *Pascendi Gregis*, p 66.
34. John S Spong, from his book *Into the Whirlwind*, quoted in *The American Church*, p 51.
35. Mary Daly, *Beyond God the Father* quoted in *Laughter of Aphrodite*, op., cit. p 140
36. Mary Daly, "After the Death of God", *Womanspirit Rising*, p 54.
37. John M Cammett, *Antonio Gramschi and the Origins of Italian Communism*, Stamford, California, Stamford University Press, 1967, p 49.
38. The Liturgical Commission, "The Language of Our Worship", pamphlet, The

Episcopal Diocese of New York, Pentecost, 1984.
39. Carroll E Simcox, "Traduttori, Traditori: Translators, Traitors", *The Christian Challenge*, June 1985.
40. F Earle Fox, "Two Ways of Looking", *The Evangelical Catholic*, XIII, No 11, August 1990, p 1.
41. *Ibid.*
42. Malcolm Boyd, *Gay Priests: An Inner Journey*, New York, St Martin's, 1986, p 68.
43. Carter Heywood, *op. cit.*, p 3.
44. Joseph P Farrell and B W Anderson, *The Pattern of Apostasy: Essays on the Collapse and Recovery of Confessionally Orthodox Christianity*, unpublished, p 9.
45. Jervis Anderson, *op. cit.*, p 90.
46. Jim Lamacchia, "The Morality of Homosexual Acts: A Reconsideration", *The St Luke's Journal of Theology*, XXXIV, No.1, December 1990, (University of South Sewanee), pp 22 and 26.
47. Murray L Newman, "Good News, Better News, Best News", *Virginia Seminary Journal*, XLII, No 3, December 1990, p 10.
48. "From the Rector", St Stephen's Anglican Church, Athens, Georgia, December 1990, p 1.
49. Alzina Stole Dale, Letter to the editor, *The Living Church*, December 9, 1990, p 3.

Six:

In the image of God

There is no Christianity without the Icon

Yves Dubois

The place of men and women in the Orthodox Church and the controversial topic of ordination of women have been the subject of two reports by the Orthodox Church world-wide: Athens 1978 and Rhodes 1988. Those documents, addressing themselves primarily to the members of the Orthodox Church, assume a basic knowledge of the teaching of the Orthodox Church on human nature, manhood and womanhood, and ministerial priesthood. This article quotes substantially from the two documents. Misunderstandings are easily created in this emotive issue: the balance has to be kept between two assertions: men and women have the same human nature; men and women are different and complementary. People get understandably anxious when they fear that in the Church one or the other of these assertions obscures the other.

In these pages, a central aspect of Orthodox theology has been emphasised: the image, or icon of God in the human race. From the early centuries of the Christian era, Orthodox Christians have used icons in their churches and in their homes as reminders of the proximity of heaven, and of the transfiguring nature of God's grace. Whether one thinks of the human vocation in general, or of the ministerial priesthood in particular, the Orthodox Tradition puts a special emphasis on the role of people as icons. I have given a deliberately provocative subtitle to this article: "There is

87

no Christianity without the Icon". I believe that if this could be acknowledged throughout Christendom, many crises and problems would be resolved.

An icon does not depict the human body in a style particular to some countries or the individual taste of a given artist. It is shown, not in its fallen state, but transfigured by the grace of God. Icons, like the Bible and the liturgical texts, express God's revelation and not the private understanding of people who may be inspired by an outlook which is not that of the Gospel. An icon is not a decoration, but a declaration and depicts what the Orthodox Church says to every human being: you are called to be a living icon, an image of God transfigured by his grace.

An Orthodox Christian looks for the image of God in every human face. Similarly, the hierarchy in the Orthodox Church is first required to provide a glimpse of the presence of the Lord Jesus among his people. This speaks to us about human dignity and the high understanding Christianity has of human nature. But it does far more: it leads us to a reflection on God's revelation of himself to Israel and to the Church, which we can read about in our Bibles. The greatest danger for Christians today is to lose sight of God's revelation of himself. If people do not begin by a study of those images, those icons, God gives of himself in the Bible, they will certainly go wrong in their understanding of human beings as images of God. They will lower the level on which they argue the case for or against the ordination of women to the priesthood. Some people oppose the ordination of women to the priesthood but mistakenly take the legalistic line that Tradition does not allow us to do this, although we are not sure why. This is extremely unsatisfactory, since it imposes a major discrimination against women with no attempt to relate it either to God's revelation about himself, or to his revelation about human nature. Those who favour the ordination of women because they do not see any theological reason against it, just want to see an end to a social discrimination; this would be right if worship were not radically affected by the gender of the person ordained to the ministerial priesthood.

Some chapters in the Bible suddenly bring us into the immediate presence of the Lord: Ezekial 1:4-28; Isaiah 6:1-4; Exodus 19:3-24; Mark 9:2-13; Revelation 1:12-18. If these chapters are accepted as central to God's revelation, to our religion, then in actual practice all our major decisions will be affected by one criterion: am I on my way towards, or away from, the Vision of God?

The Orthodox Church has a "mystical theology": i.e. a theology which makes this Vision of God central to everything. This is why the Orthodox Church considers it so important that Christians should believe that God's grace active within us is *uncreated grace*, i.e. God's own life, God's own uncreated energies permeating human beings.

We can believe in a personal and transcendent God, in life after death, in the resurrection of the body, but merely as "articles of faith", realities which do not concern us in this life. We can find Christians like that today: their beliefs are "conservative", and they do not realise how much they are swayed by secular opinion around them. They are likely to be the people who argue against the ordination of women to the priesthood on the ground of the "authority of Tradition, but with no understandable reason".

More frequently, we meet Christians who leave the ultimate destiny of mankind out of their considerations altogether. This has been a determining factor in discussions about the place of women in the Church in recent years, I believe. Everything is looked at from the point of view of social opportunities on earth. Without denying the importance of social justice within the Church, one has to point to the danger of a secularised Christianity, where the only achievements are earthly ones.

Without due consideration for what happens after death in heaven, and after the general resurrection and the last judgement, people are left with secular humanism painted over with a thin veneer of religiosity. Of course this is the major problem with much of the contemporary "Christian" scene: it has lost God, it has lost the Gospel, although it is rather shy in admitting it frankly.

I would like to argue in this article that an extremely forceful faith in the centrality of the Vision of God in Christianity by no means leads to socially conservative attitudes towards the role of women in society and in the Church. What does this centrality of the Vision of God and of the Image, Icon of God in us, have to tell us about the human nature which is common to all people, and the specific characteristics of men and women? I believe it leads us to staggering changes in Church life as we know it at the moment.

Men and Women are equally in the Image of God

The Orthodox faith is based on the revelation of God and the biblical text remains the heart of the Tradition of the Orthodox Church. An important part of the process of our salvation is the refashioning of the human mind by the divine word, the inspired text of the Bible. It is not for fallen man to re-interpret God's revelation to make it suit his passing opinions. People are in an unnatural state until they have been refashioned by the grace of the Lord Jesus. Once people have received their adoption as sons and daughters of God the Father, the Holy Spirit begins to transform their minds, opening them to the truth of the biblical revelation.

The complete equality of men and women is asserted unequivocally at the beginning of the Bible: "God said: 'Let us make man in our image, after our likeness; and let them have dominion over the fish of the sea, and over the birds of the air, and over the cattle, and over all the earth, and over every creeping thing that creeps upon the earth'. So God created man in his own image, in the image of God he created him; male and female he created them".

In Galatians 3:28, we see that for those who are in Christ, there cannot remain any inequality of the sexes due to the fallen state of this world: "There is neither Jew nor Greek, there is neither slave nor free, there is neither male nor female; for you are all one in Christ Jesus".

The 1988 report of the Orthodox Church reasserts this major aspect of her teaching:

Because of the divine revelation, which is centred upon the incarnation of the Lord, the Orthodox would affirm the following features as central to our understanding of men and women. Firstly, God is the creator of both men and women. Each has his or her origin with God. This conviction is further strengthened by our acknowledgement that Christ has come to save men and woman equally and to restore both men and women to fellowship with God (Colossians 1:20).

Of equal significance is the Orthodox conviction expressed throughout the Scriptures and Tradition of the Church that there is a distinction between the male and the female which is rooted in the very act of creation (Genesis 1:27). This distinction does not imply any form of inferiority or superiority before God. On the contrary, it is a distinction established by God Himself as part of His divine plan. Salvation does not involve, therefore, the denial of our identity as women and men but rather its transfiguration.

Witnessing the tragic dehumanisation which we often encounter in society, the Orthodox are bound to affirm in the strongest possible way the dignity of the human person, both the female and the male. Any act which denies the dignity of the human person, created in the image and likeness of God (Genesis 1:26).

In our own Western society, the Orthodox Church is confronted not merely with a materialism but with large Christian communities which have lost the sense of spiritual realities: thinly veiled unbelief and cultivated ambiguity between a secular humanist and genuinely Christian faith characterise much of Western Christendom. Two unacceptable reactions to that secularism have arisen in recent years: the neo-paganism of the New Age Movement and some authoritarian (and misogynist?) American evangelical movements. The Orthodox Church is therefore aware that the proper Christian understanding of human nature is being threatened in many different ways.

Women's interests are not necessarily best defended by those who share the views of strident feminists in the West. Neither are women best off in societies which deprive them of many basic human rights, as was the case in some countries for thousands of years. The whole question of the role of women should not stem from a negative reaction to abuses and bad situations, wherever they happen. Injustice must be countered, and women must have their very specific nature recognised. It is necessary to oppose social unfairness. Human dignity demands more than the suppression of injustice: men and women are called to share God's life! First of all, let us look at some historical legacies which have created actual social conditions contrary to Christian principles.

Historical Distortions

In the early centuries, the Church was clearly aware that the customary legal disadvantages imposed on women were sub-Christian. Nevertheless many Church regulations adopted these very restrictions against women *whilst deploring them as an unfortunate consequence of the state of society.* For instance, a woman was more severely punished than a man for sexual offences, and in the case of marriage breakdown, she was more at a disadvantage than a man would be. Not all those distortions have yet been eradicated from the Canon Law of the Orthodox Church. In her 1988 report, the Church recognises that some "feminist" complaints within Orthodox communities are completely justified:

It is necessary to confess in honesty and with humility that owing to human weakness and sinfulness, the Christian communities have not always and in all places been able to counteract effectively ideas, manners and customs, historical developments and social conditions which have resulted in practical discrimination against women. Human sinfulness has thus led to practices which do not reflect the true nature of the Church of Jesus Christ.

. . . Not all the issues raised by the feminist movement are theological issues. Some of them are social issues clothed in seemingly "theological" formulations.

The 1978 Athens Report clearly sets the question of the place of women in the Church in the perspective of human fulfilment in the Kingdom of God:

The Orthodox Church honours a woman, the Holy Virgin Mary, the Theotokos, as the human person closest to God. In the Orthodox Tradition, women saints are given such titles as Great Martyr and Equal to the Apostles. Thus it is clear that in no sense does the Orthodox Church consider women to be intrinsically inferior in God's eyes.

The Orthodox Church, no less than all other Christian bodies, has before her the duty to eliminate from her midst all social attitudes which belittle women. Christianity has something built into it – the sense that all human beings without distinction are made in the image of God – which dismantles macho attitudes. Every human face without exception is called to see the Vision of God and to reflect the Face of God. Christians must proclaim this in word, in social attitudes, in their teaching, and local Church communities should have this as their first responsibility.

In the case of the Orthodox, nationalism even more than sexism often mars the life of many Church communities. We need not only to eliminate sinful attitudes, but also to activate the full potential of our people, men, women and children. The Church is not meant to include passive participants, of whom little is required and to whom little responsibility needs to be given. Much "traditionalism" has nothing to do with the Gospel or the Faith of the Church. What good is it to preserve traditional appearances which can indeed be a hindrance to God's grace, to the action of the Holy Spirit? Every suggestion leading to a greater fulfilment of God's will must be examined on its own merit: will it lead people more towards the Vision of God?

It would seem to me that, in the Orthodox Church, some "revolutionary" steps need to be taken urgently: parishes need a team of deacons, female as well as male with wide-ranging pastoral and teaching competence. We need an army of teachers of both sexes to teach the Bible, to train people in their personal prayer, in their moral responsibilities. We need thoroughly Christian doctors, nurses, social workers, lawyers, politicians, of both sexes, so that the world may not be led rapidly by the godless to its spiritual, moral and physical destruction, as seems at present to be the case. Is it spiritually healthy to say: "Because we have an exlusively male priesthood, we are automatically leading mankind to the Vision of God"?

In many Christian communities, the understanding of God and of the Church has been poor and distorted for a very long time. People seem to have forgotten that every baptised Christian is an adoptive son or daughter of God the Father, meant to have a warm personal relationship with the most loving Father. They do not seem to know that every Christian is a member of Christ, meant to have one life with Jesus and with the other members of his Body; he or she, by unction with the holy Chrism, has been anointed with the Holy Spirit, and ought to manifest the gifts and fruit of the Spirit. Yet many do not have that relationship or even any notion of it. They have lost the sense of the Image of God, the Icon, the Vision of God. And there is no Christianity if there is no icon!

As a consequence, they see the Church not as the Body of Jesus, but as an administrative machinery, often solely identified with the clergy. Many members of the clergy, who have no attraction for theological liberalism, are quite content with the dull routine of an ecclesiastical civil service, and hardly attempt to foster in their flock a living relationship with the Holy Trinity. Christianity for the majority in such communities means (and has meant for centuries) loyalty to the ecclesiastical machinery and basic good manners, little more. No wonder those people ask: why not have women priests? Surely if a woman can be an excellent civil servant, she can also be a priest or minister?

The step from dead traditionalism to liberalism is minute: both positions stem from a lack of proper teaching and proper experience of God. Ignorance and religious minimalism make people insensitive to the grossest theological mistakes. In all Churches and denominations, many people who think of themselves as "traditionalists" know very little about their Christian faith. They fear change not because they perceive clearly an imminent theological danger, but because they have so little grasp of the basics of Christianity that any change might shatter everything in their religion. They retire into a shell instead of responding to Jesus' parable of the Sower by receiving the Word and putting it into practice. Sooner or later their religion will collapse and they will join the "liberals" who shrug their shoulders at the idea of any definite revelation from God.

Frequently, Christians in the Catholic and Protestant traditions imagine that the Orthodox Church is a mummified Byzantine relic with no life and no flexibility in it. This is a gross caricature of a Church for whom Tradition means not custom but the living guidance of the Holy Spirit. What is important for the Orthodox Church is faithfulness to Christ and his Gospel, irrespective of social fashions: nothing in the Church should be decided on the basis of a bias for either old-fashioned or avant-garde social ideas. Especially in this century, many Christians have been led astray by a fascination for social and political ideologies, either of a so-called right-wing or left-wing nature.

The New Paganism and its Old Parent

We have just seen that according to the Orthodox Church, each person is called to be a living icon, a transfigured image of God. Every human being is equally called to deification by the grace of God: that is enough to establish that every person, from the unborn child to the head of state, is of equal worth before God. Alongside this fundamental truth, each person has a unique differentiated role. A man is not a woman; a Jew is not a Gentile; a bishop is not a catechumen. Each has a special gift: the basic human nature is common, the specific gift is not.

When Saint Paul speaks of man being the glory of God, but woman the glory of man, he is not talking of the relative worth of male or female persons. He is reminding his readers that maleness is an image, an icon, a symbol of the Fatherhood of God, and femaleness is an image, icon, symbol of the whole of mankind.

God has built into his creation the male and female genders for more reasons than just biological procreation. In human terms, maleness becomes fatherhood, a relationship much richer in significance than its mere biological aspect. A child needs a father not only to be conceived. The psychological and social aspects of fatherhood all require a man: a woman is never quite a father. All this naturally produces an imagery which fits God's relationship with his creation.

On the other hand, femininity is a natural symbol of "Mother-Earth", of the creation. A man cannot ever be a "mother", in the psychological and social senses as well as the biological.

Maleness means fatherhood: this enables it to serve as an icon of the transcendent God. It has always been obvious to anyone of biblical faith, whether Jew or Christian, that God is not made in a biological sense. It is also obvious that maleness does not make a person closer to God. In their own relationship with God, all male human beings are part of creation, and are in a "female" relationship with God.

Because of this basic symbolism within creation, a female priesthood must be a cult of "Mother-Earth". It has no choice: it will be fertility orientated, pantheistic and pagan, because it is a basic reflex of human nature to consider priests or priestesses as images of the Divine. In a religion with priestesses, the "Vision" of Ezekiel, Isaiah, Moses and the book of Revelation is automatically eliminated and replaced by the imagery of paganism. This is borne out by the experience of American so-called Christian feminism. It has led to the rewriting of the Bible and the liturgical texts (exclusively in non-Orthodox Churches) in a way which blurs any masculine reference to God. There has been a logical progression from the ordination of women to the replacement of the image of God the Father completely or partially by female imagery and vocabulary; gradually, New Age paganism takes over. Needless to say, no Orthodox Christian could treat as fellow-Christians people who have departed from the biblical revelation of God.

Because the Church, the bishop or priest is an icon of Christ, who is himself the icon of the Father (Colossians 1:15, "He is the icon of the invisible God, the firstborn over all creation"), only men can be ordained to the priesthood.

A Christian or a Jew can say that God loves us like a mother; they must say that God is not a sexual being, that he does not procreate as a pagan god does. Neither Jew nor Christian can ever address God in prayer as "Mother". This would be the end of Judaism and Christianity, because the cult of the Mother-Goddess is always a worship of the created universe.

The Orthodox Church emphasises that the male ministerial priesthood reflects the Fatherhood of God. Orthodoxy is equally emphatic about the equal worth of women and men. On the other hand, ancient Mediterranean society socially demeaned women to a brutal extent, but had priestesses for its pagan rites centred on cults of a mother-goddess.

If the Orthodox teaching on the iconographic nature of the

sexes were rejected, then there would be no reason whatever against the ordination of women to the priesthood. When feminists claim that a biblical teaching on the religious symbolism of male-female duality downgrades women in favour of men, they misunderstand the Bible altogether. This misunderstanding stems from a secularised reading of the Bible which has lost the basic mystical sense common to Judaism and Christianity.

The grace of God uses the distinction between the sexes for the glorification of mankind. The two main icons found in the Orthodox Church are those of Jesus and of his Mother: the Saviour manifests all that can be known of the Godhead in his humanity; the Mother of God manifests the transfiguration of human creatures by the grace of God.

How does it work out in practice in the Church? This iconographic understanding of human nature highlights a dilemma: can the Church be both fair to women and maintain the God-given complementarity between men and women? The male monopoly in Church leadership can lead to grave abuse of authority: priests have a moral duty to function harmoniously within the whole Church community. If they lord it over the people in the way Jesus condemned, they will surely precipitate an ever-growing number of Christian communities towards the ordination of women. We read in Mark 10:42-44:

> You know that those who are regarded as rulers of the Gentiles lord it over them, and their high officials exercise authority over them. Not so with you. Instead, whoever wants to become great among you must be your servant, and whoever wants to be first must be slave of all. For even the Son of Man did not come to be served, but to serve, and to give his life as a ransom for many.

Let us turn from these general considerations to the concrete case of male and female responsibility in our contemporary parish communities.

Human Icons and Daily Christian Living
A. Male Responsibilities

All male responsibility is linked with the role of father-figure to which a man is called. This fatherly role is a reflection on earth of God the Father: it is a role of love, responsibility and leadership. It is not a role of despotic domination. What characterises God's attitude towards his rational creatures is the freedom he gives us. God asks for the love he would like to receive from us, and never compels. The love he gives us in return brings us into a share in his eternal life, or, as the apostle Peter boldly says, a share in his divine nature (II Peter 1:4).

A certain American "moral majority" movement has identified in recent years restoring male responsibility with reinstating an oppressive domineering attitude on the part of fathers in families and of clergy in Churches. Their stance is a caricature of the Christian attitude.

There is no place within the Christian community for the boorishly bossy who ignore actual persons and actual situations, be they men or women. A healthy community must be like a loving family, where people truly cooperate with each other. The father of a family listens to his wife and does not assume he is wiser than her. The parish priest and the Bishop teach but also listen: they do not have a monopoly on the Holy Spirit!

For some time, the whole Orthodox Church has talked about restoring in every parish one or two deacons and deaconesses. While such a healthy and urgently needed step would in my view prevent a feminist crisis within the Orthodox Church, it is even more important that every parish should encourage all its members to exercise a very full Christian ministry, under the guidance of the priest. Men, women and children can spread the Gospel, pray with and over the sick, pray with and help in many ways people of all ages and situations. There should be no parishes where people feel they wish they were priests so they can have some status! Harmony and unity in the family and parish are essential: much feminism today stems from a lack of human warmth within Christian communities.

It is of the essence of biblical thought that the Lord created Adam: mankind is one; woman was not created as a different species, but taken out of Adam. The rejection of the word "mankind" is dangerous because it necessarily leads, not to greater equality and unity, but to a radical separation between men and women. It is not to be regretted that the English language uses the word "man" both for the male of the species, and also for "human being" of either sex: this emphasises the fact that mankind is one. We need to get away from the recently-developed over-sensitivity to the supposedly "sexist" contents of the words "mankind" and "man".

B. Female Responsibilities

The 1988 report gives substantial teaching on the role of women:

> The central person in the special ministry of women in the divine plan of salvation is the Theotokos, the Mother of God. In her is fulfilled the special work of the Holy Spirit for the incarnation of the Son and Word of God . . . The Church, like the Theotokos receives the Holy Spirit, through whose energy both Christ is born and also the children of the new humanity in Christ are brought into the world.

Women have been endowed in their nature with a special gift of love, of the gift of themselves to God: the Mother of God is their prototype. Every woman is called to remind the whole of society that human fulfilment is first in personal depth and authenticity, and only secondarily in outward status. Outward status can be deceptive: what a person is matters more than any official and institutional rank.

Women have a most important and prophetic ministry:

their calling to assert that a personal, moral authority is ultimately more important than an institutional status. Institutionalised prophesy is a contradiction: the church needs to remind herself constantly of the prophetic value of the moral authority of women, of their non-involvement in the priestly hierarchy.

Prophetic roles often mean poverty in worldly terms, balanced with wealth in spiritual terms. This is not the exclusive possession of women: Jesus took that road of poverty as well as his Mother; the Saints of the Church, like the Sages of Israel, chose to be the Poor of God.

In the Orthodox Church, parish priests are married: among the Slavs, a priest's wife is called "Matushka"(Mother); among the Greeks, a priest's wife is called "Presvytera". Their motherly authority and their pastoral role in the parish, very different from the authority of the priest, are considerable. There is no doubt that in the Orthodox Church, the obvious role of the priest's wife contributes towards the absence of a loud demand for the ordination of women.

Women are first and foremost responsible for the actual life of the Body of Christ. Their great responsibility is to declericalise the Church: the clergy rightly represent the head, Christ. But a head without a body is not a live being any more than a body without a head. If the Church and activity within the Church become identified with the clergy, then you are left with a formalist, dead institution. This happens among the Orthodox, although probably less than among other Christians. The women as lay people, are responsible for activating the Body. Let me quote from the 1988 report:

> The manifestations of the Kingdom of God is inaugurated in the Church and through the Church, as the historic Body of Christ, into which all the faithful are incorporated as members, and as such are constituted the People of God.
>
> As members of the one and the same body, the faithful are united with each other and with the divine Head of

the Body through divine grace in the new life in Christ. Through this they live the new reality as a continuous communion with the Triune God, thus becoming 'a chosen race, a royal priesthood, a holy nation' (I Peter 2:9). All of the members of the Church share in the prophetic, high priestly and royal office of Christ. They become through divine grace communicants of all the blessings of divine glory by their adoption. They live the fullness of the divinely revealed truth in the Church, and do obtain the experience of the variety of the gifts of the Holy Spirit in the mystical (sacramental) life of the membership of the Church.

The Holy Spirit was given to the Church so that it could unite those who are divided by different races and conditions. For the aged and the young, the poverty – stricken and the wealthy, the infant and the adolescent, the woman and the man, every soul becomes one thing in the body of the Church. Thus, in the mystery of the Church, the faithful are interconnected and, as an unbroken body, they create the Paschal and Pentecostal Mystery of Christ.

The Ecumenical Dimension

Because Orthodox Christians live alongside other Christians, they cannot consider the issue of the roles of men and women in their Church as if ideas and events in other Churches and denominations did not exist.

Protestant Denominations

The issue of the ordination of women has given the Orthodox Church the opportunity to remind Anglican and other Christians that apostolic succession is not merely a question of outward gestures, but of genuine apostolic faith. The Athens 1978 Report says:

The action of ordaining women to the priesthood involves

not simply a canonical point of Christian discipline, but the basis of the Christian faith as expressed in the Church's ministries . . . the apostolic succession is not merely continuity in the outward laying on of hands, but signifies continuity in apostolic faith and spiritual life.

The rejection by Protestantism of a ministerial priesthood has led to a weakening of the centrality in worship and life of the biblical theme of the Vision of God. It has altogether disappeared in Christian communities which have been taken over by theological liberalism. The Anglican Church is about to experience a major upheaval over the issue of the ordination of women: Catholic-minded Anglicans sense that this will have a very negative effect on their Church in the direction of further playing down liturgical participation in the heavenly worship around the Throne of God.

Conservative Evangelical Christians deserve admiration for their devotion to the Bible as the inspired Word of God and their tireless dedication to evangelism: many Orthodox would learn much from them. On the other hand, their rejection of a ministerial priesthood, which leads many (not all) of them to back the idea of the ordination of women, could have consequences they may not fully realise.

The Bible conveys truth through verbal symbols, verbal icons. It can be dangerous to be allergic to the use of liturgical symbols. People risk losing the Bible, the Word of God, if they do not keep hold of the importance and effectiveness of symbols. The Bible's verbal images are both symbol and simple fact, as in the statement "the Church is the body of Christ, and Christ is the head of the Church".

The relationship between husband and wife within the family, and between priest as father-image and parish community, are real-life biblical symbols of God's relationship with his Church, of Christ's relationship with his Church. We should never undervalue or tamper with the apostolic ministry, or with the God-given sexual

103

differentiations: they are too close to the biblical foundations of our faith.

In this age of theological liberalism, the discovery of orthodox Judaism could play an important role in preserving a proper understanding of the Bible among Christians, and especially among Evangelicals. It is indicative that today, orthodox Jews print most of the Bible commentaries worth reading! A little acquaintance with their culture makes one aware of the centrality of the Jerusalem Temple in their lives; their preservation of specific male and female roles does not lead to the oppression of women, in spite of popular caricature. Finally they can teach us again the importance of the Commandments. Christians should take the trouble to familiarise themselves with orthodox Jewish commentaries, Prayer Books and piety. It would restore a proper understanding of the Vision of God.

The Roman Catholic Church

I will not deal here with the influences on many Catholic circles of theological liberalism and the inter-faith movement. These cause the Orthodox Church's deepest worries in her relationship with Roman Catholics. What has been said about the Protestant world also applies to those Catholics affected by similar trends.

Catholic theology shares a similar sense of tradition with the Orthodox Church. The difference between us is often quite subtle, and yet important. The theology of ministerial priesthood is one instance of this type of difference. I believe that the Orthodox emphasis on the role of the priesthood as 'icon' has definite advantages over the Catholic emphasis on 'authority' in discussions about the ordination of women.

While Roman Catholic theology understands bishops and presbyters to be Christ's *representatives* on earth, the Orthodox Church sees them as his *representation*. There is here an important difference of emphasis. Perhaps both Catholics and Orthodox ought to make greater efforts to listen to each other in this as in other aspects of the Faith.

A representative replaces someone, stands in for someone who is not personally present. The representative is the one mouthpiece of a person, whose authority he has inherited. Ultimately, in Roman Catholic theology, the Pope is Christ's Vicar on earth: this makes him inevitably infallible, and it gives him immediate jurisdiction over all Christians, since he is invested with the power to stand in for Christ himself.

The Orthodox could never accept the Latin position on the role of the papacy, but the Orthodox episcopate could at times learn something from the forceful leadership of some of the best Catholic hierarchs. The Orthodox Church has never denied to the Pope of Rome the role he had in the early centuries, and which remains enshrined in Orthodox Canon law from the time of the Seven Ecumenical Councils.

Orthodox theology from the earliest centuries has never viewed the Pope or any other hierarch as invested with the authority of Christ's actual Vicar, or stand-in, on earth. All hierarchs are seen in Orthodox theology as icons of Christ: Christ himself rules through his Gospel, through his Holy Spirit. The bishops, including patriarchs and popes, are there to proclaim the Gospel of Christ and the Tradition of the Church.

The Holy Spirit empowers the clergy to proclaim the truth, and the ability to recognise the truth. The charisma of the laity is a receptive and discriminating one: not only does it receive and live the teaching proclaimed, but it also evaluates whether the hierarchy are in fact proclaiming Christ's teaching, the Apostles' teaching, the Tradition of the Church, or whether they are misusing their position, teaching their own ideas, departing from Orthodoxy. The laity often receives important prophetic gifts.

It would seem that in the Orthodox Church the importance of being the Bride, the Church who responds to the proclamation of the truth of Christ, her Bridegroom, is more forcefully stressed. It is the actual life of the community

105

which matters. Directives, teaching, proclaiming, acquire substance when the body of the faithful live accordingly. The people's participation at the Liturgy is what justifies its celebration. The Holy Spirit in the heart of the faithful is what justifies the Church structures. The Orthodox Church has a deep sense of the importance of the feminine role, and sees the right balance between the masculine and feminine aspects of life as most important for the reunion of Christendom.

Conclusion

Christ is the Revelation of the Father and the Head of the Church. Only a profound renewal of personal relationship with Jesus as Lord of our lives can heal our outlook on the role of men and women in the Church and in society. We understand Jesus by becoming icons of Jesus.

The Mother of God is the embodiment of mankind receiving the Word of God, receiving deifying grace. Only a close relationship with her can heal the hearts of those who feel wounded by society. Only a real understanding of her person, her place in the Bible, in the history of salvation, will heal the rift between Christians, and tensions between the sexes.

Both men and women have to embody something of the icon of Christ and of the icon of the Mother of God: every person has to reveal God to the world and receive his grace.

But in the priestly hierarchy of the Church, only men can reflect Jesus, as Father-image. It is difficult to understand how the exclusion of women from the priestly hierachy can lead to tensions provided there is a healthy Church community and a genuinely active "priesthood of all believers" shared by all persons of either sex.

Seven:

Goddesses of their own making

Pat Taylor

Feminism in the Australian Church

In the 1980s two strong movements of feminists emerged: 'Women-Church' and 'Women and the Australian Church' (WATAC), the latter functioning in "a consciousness-raising role among Catholic women in general" These two movements are part of a large, public and very active community of women and men found in many countries of the western world. In 1989-90 two large conferences organised by the Movement for the Ordination of Women (MOW), Women-Church and WATAC were held in New South Wales. Over 450 women attended. These groups are currently engaged in two related tasks: discovering and creating both a female-centred mythology and a mythology representing male-female mutuality.

What is meant by a 'female-centred mythology'? Here, in a definition of freedom, as quoted in *Knowing otherwise - Feminism, Women and Religion* by Erin White and Marie Tulip, we have it clarified:

> . . . to discover a *female-centred* theology – one in which we are not subordinate to males . . . (males throughout the book always include God Himself) but one in which we are our own *centred-selves*.[1] (italics added)

Contrast this to Christ's definition of freedom:

> If you hold to my teaching you are really my disciples. Then you will know the truth and the truth will set you free.[2]

107

At the outset of their book, White and Tulip make a statement which is perhaps more revealing than they are aware. They say that post-Christian feminists today are increasingly challenging the "patriarchal God of Christianity and Judaism" because they "no longer find that Christianity meets their experience".[3] Has Christianity ever, in fact, been experienced by these women? There is certainly no evidence, or even mention throughout the book of a personal relationship with Jesus Christ – indeed the theme running through it is one of self-identified women, and women-identified men – and Christianity constantly referred to as a myth (particularly, of course, the first three chapters of Genesis).

The writings of feminist theologian and biblical scholar Elisabeth Schussler Fiorenze, one of the leaders of Women-Church, are frequently quoted – indeed applauded throughout the book. Fiorenze associates God with the "female divine wisdom, Sophia" and says:

> Jesus probably understood himself as the prophet and child of Sophia.[4]

As a so-called biblical scholar, one must wonder what Bible she was studying. There seems no doubt whatsoever in the New Testament, that Jesus knew exactly who he was, where he had come from and where he was going. However, Fiorenze goes on to say:

> Sophia is a people-loving spirit who shares the throne of God and that it is as *her* messenger that Jesus calls all who labour and are heavy laden and promises them rest.[5]

White and Tulip tell us that there are a multiplicity of ways in which women's spirituality is being expressed and named today. For example they invite the reader to observe the progressiveness of a 'naming' ritual devised by a local group of Women-Church in 1989, where the mother dedicates her girl-child to "the Goddess". She describes to all assembled the visit in her dreams of a white leopard who gave her a message about the child's identity. She explains she has taken her child's name Cara from Kore, an ancient name for the goddess, which apparently means "heart of the world". Throughout the ritual, the "goddess" is invoked and addressed as "mother".[6]

'Salvific' Menstruation?

In another Women-Church ritual, women stand naked around a pool, pronouncing a variety of chants to revere the menstrual cycle, and after immersing themselves three times in the pool arise to say "blessed is the dying away and blessed is the regeneration".[7] Regeneration through whom and from what?

This ritual is commended to us in a chapter entitled "The Issue of Blood" and presents an inordinate obsession with menstruation. It closes with this statement:

Blessed be women, blessed by our holy menstrual blood Women know it can redeem the world.[8]

In another chapter a feminist rages against an 'ineffectual man' who offered her communion, identifying, as she put it,

. . . with the male Jesus' shedding of blood, and proclaiming that it was done for me, when I knew it was my mother who at my birth shed blood for me.[9]

It is from statements like these that one is alerted to the true source of such "theology". Who would have a vested interest in reducing the Fall of Man as recorded in Genesis 1-3 to "myth"; in negating the significance of the shed blood of Christ; in substituting the regeneration of the individual in baptism into Christ with a "self-centred ritual"?

Jesus said to the Pharisees of his day:

Why is my language not clear to you? Because you are unable to hear what I say. You belong to your father, the devil, and you want to carry out your father's desire. He was a murderer from the beginning, not holding to the truth, for there is no truth in him.[10]

Any reminder of the shed blood of Jesus is anathema to Satan – for it was this that forgave our sin, continues to cleanse us from sin, and defeated the power of the evil one over us for ever. The first three chapters of Genesis give us the clues to Satan's existence, character, purposes and strategy, and his prophesied defeat by the seed of the woman. Any doubt cast on the deity of Christ, the unique God-Man, has always been a favourite ploy of his.

The Virtue of Vice

Feminist theology denounces the way in which 'traditional' Christianity has repeatedly called us to practise the virtues of humility, meekness, obedience and purity, and to repent of pride, anger, impurity and lust. They argue that in Western culture the latter are predominantly 'male' sins, women being 'innocent' of them. White and Tulip tell us that feminist theologians have now renamed traditional virtues as sinful for women, because they only have "the effect of entrenching women in their own subordination and male domination".[11] Feminists have redefined humility, obedience and purity as female sins and pride, anger and lust as female virtues.

It is frightening to see the parallels between the emphases in this Australian book and the teaching of 'Starhawk', a self-confessed witch employed by Mathew Fox, OP at the Institute for Culture and Creation Spirituality in California. Her teachings and influence are being introduced as 'Creation Spirituality' through churches, using small groups and communities and religious education centres.[12] New Zealand's Cecily Sheehy, OP and Sr Monica Green, RSM of Australia have both studied under Starhawk and Fox.

Here is an example of Starhawk's theology:

The mythology of Christ has certainly been used as much as any ideology in history to support oppression and the status quo . . . at this moment in history, the mythology

110

and imagery of the Goddess carry special liberating power. They free us from the domination of the all-male God who has so strongly legitimized male rule, and by extension all systems of domination.[13]

Take note too of Fr Mathew Fox's 'Creation Spirituality':

The idea of a private salvation is utterly obsolete . . . the cosmic Christ can be both female and male, heterosexual and homosexual . . . I believe there is a need to recover the sense of both lust and chastity as powers and therefore virtues within all people . . .[14]

The Movement for the Ordination of Women has linked itself with Women-Church and WATAC, and White and Tulip state that their common efforts are in many struggles, viz. women's right to choose in the area of abortion; lesbian and gay liberation; Aboriginal rights and the rights for women from other cultures; and the peace movement. A constructive effect, they say, of their combined campaign is that the women involved have acquired a 'much deeper' theological and biblical understanding and will be in a better position to

. . . subvert patriarchal styles and structures when they are eventually ordained. The ordination issue is only the tip of the iceberg.[15]

Re-intepretation and Rationalisation

To achieve their aims feminists are fostering a body of feminist scholarship in Australia, which now extends across various disciplines, to be found in books, research papers, journals and so on, and much of it is being disseminated through Women's Studies courses. Significant numbers of feminists now occupy leadership positions in areas of public and professional life. Erin White is post-doctoral Fellow in the School of Philosophy at the University of New South Wales and co-editor of a journal of feminist studies in religion called *Women-Church*. Marie Tulip teaches courses in feminism and religion and contemporary women's poetry.

She worked on the Commission on the Status of Women of the Australian Council of Churches.

The whole 'equality' issue in the Christian church has become confused. Pivotal in the 'christian' feminists' arguments is the verse from Galatians 3:28, which in true context, has no relevance to the validity of female church leaders. Paul is pointing out here that "in Christ" all are equal heirs of salvation. "In Christ" we all become, as it were, Abraham's seed, and therefore able to receive the eternal promises. Having established that fact, it is also Paul who emphatically re-states God's divine order in the family and the church, not (as feminists would have us believe) because of his cultural thinking, but taking us back to Creation and Genesis for his authority.

It will be to our detriment if we challenge God's order for the New Testament church in this way. Too much re-interpretation and rationalization has gone on already in an attempt to 'fit' the scriptures with our 'enlightened' twentieth century, and anything we find 'unacceptable' today. For those who persist in thinking that women are second rate citizens of God's kingdom, there are two scriptural principles:

1. God has ascribed honour to the place of subordination. This is part of the reason the husband is commanded to honour his wife in I Peter 3:7.

2. It is pride and rebellion against God that moves Christian women to refuse to fulfil their positions in marriage and the church. This rebellion is part of the judgement in Genesis 3:16.

But Biblical feminists speak in the names of equality, not pride – and justice, not rebellion. It is God alone who determines what justice is. Therefore it is fair and just that women cannot be elders in the church, even though an equal partnership of the sexes in marriage and in the church may seem like a better idea to many people.

Of course, church leaders have often been guilty of the

112

wrong emphasis on the Bible's true teaching. Churches have been male dominated rather than directed with suppressed rather than expressed womanhood. However, subjective reaction to such wrong cannot be accommodated when it swings to an opposite extreme.

Once true biblical convictions have been reached, what can be done? David Pawson, author of *Leadership is Male,* [16] suggests that more opportunities for women's ministries must be opened up through the church. Many Christian women who accept that biblical leadership is male, rightly complain that avenues of ministry have been unnecessarily inhibited by male monopoly – and by this writer's experience, the charge is often justified.

The second step that Pawson suggests is that the church must strive to train its men for leadership. The answer to the present imbalance is not to weaken women's contribution he says, but to strengthen the men's. Local churches must give a high priority to evangelising and disciplining men, as Jesus did. It's better to teach a man to love and lead his wife and family, Pawson states, than provide women's meetings and youth clubs to compensate for Godless fathers. It's very wrong to deny leadership to women, while doing little or nothing about training men for this responsibility.

When we question God's word and are tempted to tamper with it, what, or whom are we really questioning? Are we tempted to think that God doesn't understand women today? Didn't he know how educated women would be today? Psalm 33:11 says

> The Counsel of the Lord stands forever, the thoughts of His heart to all generations.

The education and emancipation of women has not taken God by surprise. The situations and circumstances women find themselves in today were not outside His knowledge when His word was written. He came to our creation with timeless intelligence, standing outside time and culture –

the Alpha and Omega. To concede that the scriptures – any portion of them – contain error, contradiction or irrelevant culturally determined opinions of its human authors leads to serious consequences. It produces uncertainty and doubts about the other doctrines of the faith and about the very character of God Himself – and then to whom do we turn? The feminists have turned to goddesses of their own making.

REFERENCES

1. Erin White, Marie Tulip, *Knowing Otherwise - Feminism, Women and Religion*, Victoria, David Lovell Publishing, 1991, p 161.
2. John 8:31-36.
3. *Op., cit.*, p viii.
4. *Op., cit.*, p 20.
5. *Op., cit.*
6. *Op., cit.*, pp135,136.
7. *Op., cit.*
8. *Op., cit.*
9. *Op., cit.*, p 28.
10. John 8:43,44.
11. *Op., cit.*, p 51.
12. Reported in *Time (Australia) Magazine*, 6 May 1991, and *Fidelity*, Newsletter of John XXIII Fellowship, September 1990.
13. Starhawk, *Truth and Dare*, New York, Harper and Row, 1990, pp 20,21.
14. Fr Mathew Fox, OP, *The Coming of the Cosmic Christ*, Melbourne, Collins Dove, 1990.
15. White and Tulip, *op., cit.*, p xi.
16. David Pawson, *Leadership is Male*, Crowborough, Highland Books, 1988.
17. Elizabeth Elliot, address entitled "Spiritual Motherhood", given at the Philosophy of Christian Womanhood National Leaders' Conference, 1988.

Note: *Goddesses of Their Own Making* is an edited version of an article by Pat Taylor entitled "Feminism in the Church", in *Endeavour Forum*, Newsletter No 62, August 1991, Victoria, Australia.

Eight

From Convent to Coven

A book review by Babette Francis

Ungodly Rage: The Hidden Face of Catholic Feminism
by Donna Steichen, San Francisco, Ignatius Press, 1991.

Donna Steichen is an American journalist who has documented, chronicled and analysed the progress of feminism within the North American Catholic Church.

Many have assumed that Catholic feminism is a benign movement concerned with updating the Church for contemporary society; involvement in neo-pagan rituals or witchcraft seems unimaginable. The author's investigations show that Catholic feminism suffers from all the ills of secular feminism, such as support for abortion rights, but in addition, it espouses witchcraft and Goddess-religion. What has been called the progression from convent to coven is documented in the book and the author has noted carefully themes, dates, speakers and content of papers, in order to trace the development and fruition of Catholic feminism.

The Fourth Annual *Women and Spirituality* conference in Minnesota in 1985, (always held on the weekend closest to Halloween, celebrated by many participants as *Samhain,* the festival of the dead in witchcraft) was a watershed and included most elements of neo-pagan feminism. Keynote speaker Rosemary Radford Ruether, referred to Jesus as a 'symbol' some might want to retain, and ridiculed the concept of sin, except for the "original sin" of sexism. She referred to the emerging 'Women-Church' as the "ultimate Exodus" and added:

. . . the group (Women-Church) may contain several traditions such as Christian, Jewish, Wiccan and shamanistic, but if it grows too large, it should be subdivided into . . . covens.

Another speaker Peggy Kavaney, pastoral minister at St Luke's in St Paul, advised the audience to

. . . do away with . . . the Fall-Redemption, it hasn't worked for us.

One of the workshops organised by Joan Keller-Maresh, at one time a religious sister, was entitled:

"From Convent to Coven: A Journey to the Old Religion of the Goddess".

The School Sisters of Notre Dame were heavily involved in the Conference which included an ecumenical communion service conducted by a woman minister, a feminist liturgy, and a Wiccan (witchcraft) ritual by two priestesses. A common factor was a determination amongst delegates to worship a female deity.

Dorothy Rollins, associate campus minister at St Benedict's College, Minnesota, described the conference as "reflecting an excellent value system". Following the Conference Rosemary Radford Ruether advised liberal Catholics to retain both 'autonomy' and the appearance of legitimate 'Catholicity' in its institutional power bases,

. . . as camouflage while revolutionising from within . . .
They will have far more impact both on the Church and on the world than if they were separated from it.

The advantage gained is

. . . the difference between shouting with the unaided human voice and speaking through a global system of telecommunications.

Despite the radical and anti-Church tone of these and other conferences, Steichen reported surprise on the part of delegates who had been funded by their churches and bishops. With a mixture of incredulity and satisfaction one delegate remarked:

. . . and we got our pastors to pay for us to come to this!

Steichen also noted the often 'lunatic' (pertaining to moon-goddesses) rituals of religious feminists which include such chants as:

Holy Virgin Huntress, Artemis, Artemis, Maiden come to us . . .

Margot Adler, author of *Drawing Down the Moon* was a participant at one *Women and Spirituality* conference. She pointed out that the myths are not even authentic. She said:

(revivalist witches) . . . invent their own mythic stories, unconcerned about authenticity or logical consistency . . .

Steichen concluded:

In net effect, as opposed to intent, the weekend made the most persuasive argument I have ever encountered for the superiority of patriarchy.

Not all women feminists are responsible for the idolatries of religious feminism. Rev Mathew Fox of the Institute of Culture and Creation Spirituality (ICCS) in California, provides much of the inspiration and has forged links between feminism and superstitious environmentalism. Fr Fox holds that Stone Age European societies centred on worship of Mother Earth, lived in matriarchal harmony until patriarchal males seized power some 5,000 years before Christ. Starhawk, a self-styled witch, is on Fox's faculty at ICCS. He claims the cosmological, non-dualistic, matrifocal cultures of native peoples with reverence for Mother Earth, had more advanced civilizations than European Christians. In contrast, Steven Goldberg's *The Inevitability of Patriarchy* conclusively establishes that no matriarchal society, of the kind Fox describes, ever existed or could exist.

Sr Madonna Kolbenschlag, a Mathew Fox follower, in her

117

book *Kiss Sleeping Beauty Goodbye*, alludes to witchcraft and discusses Goddess-religion as a necessary stage in an evolutionary process that is moving humanity and the 'God-who-is-coming-to-be' towards transformation in a 'New Faith'.

Every neo-pagan witch is not necessarily a feminist, nor are all religious feminists witches, but feminists make up a growing section of today's Wiccan practitioners. Steichen writes:

> Those involved are not the ignorant but the educated, of what has been called "the new Catholic knowledge class". Feminist theologians, nuns, laywomen from Catholic middle-management, especially 'peace and justice' networkers, have for 25 years in workshops, conferences and writing, fed a growing rage against male domination and have decided they will not worship a God identified as "Father" . . . They will serve only the divine within i.e. themselves. They call themselves Women-Church.

The book goes on to document the links between the feminists and the pro-abortion movement. Sr Anne Carr, BVM, member of the Board of trustees of Mandelein College, a Catholic women's college in Chicago, was one of 24 American nuns who, in 1984, signed a *New York Times* advertisement denying that there is a binding Catholic teaching on the morality of abortion. Mary Griffin, director of graduate liberal studies at Mandelein, signed a second *New York Times* advertisement, expressing solidarity with signers of the first. Sr Mary DeCock, BVM, member of the liberal studies advisory committee and teacher in graduate religious studies, also signed the second advertisement.

Not all Catholic religious feminists are nuns, but in America nuns comprise the majority of religious feminists:

> . . . entire communities from the mother house down having policies adversarial towards the Church.

Among prominent laywomen are Rosemary Radford

118

Ruether, who is married with children, and feminist theologian Elizabeth Schussler Fiorenze, a member of both Women's Ordination Conference and Catholic Committee on Pluralism and Abortion, putative sponsor of the "Catholic For Free Choice", in the 1984 *New York Times* advertisement. Another laywoman, Mary Hunt, described by Steichen as "the complete feminist theologian", founded Water, an organisation implementing an ecumenical centre for feminist strategy and ritual. Water is a member of Women-Church Convergence and Hunt is also an uncloseted lesbian.

In 1988 at St John Baptist, Schenectady, Hunt gave a talk on "Being Church in the twenty-first Century". She predicted the ordination of women, that "lesbian and gay people in church will become as common as candles", extolled remarriage after divorce, and homosexual marriage in the name of "diversity", and pointed to the fact that "my lecture was not moved off this property" despite the protests of concerned Catholics who prayed and picketed outside. A priest with the picketers said that Hunt being permitted to speak in church on Good Shepherd Sunday is

. . . like allowing the sheep to be brought to the wolf.

Steichen's observations are, she believes, only the tip of the iceberg; and that conferences she attended "were doubtless duplicated in almost any diocese". The common agenda of Catholic feminists are

. . . demands for inclusive language, innovative liturgy, feminist interpretations of spirituality, theology, doctrine and canon law, equal access to all church offices, permissiveness in regard to sexual and marital irregularities, resistance to hierarchical authority, and leftist politics. They cite standard authorities, 'The spirit of Vatican II', Mathew Fox and the corps of feminist theologians headed by Ruether.

Dr Mary Jo Weaver, associate professor of religious studies,

Indiana University, and author of *New Catholic Women,* is named with reverence among Wicca feminists. Weaver claims feminists can rewrite Scripture, enlarging or inventing female roles. The experience can give us

> . . . a profoundly enlarged understanding of biblical traditions – we are led by the logic of the process to . . . redefine theology and to articulate the divine will in its pluralistic and political modalities.

Steichen comments wryly that Weaver's perspective, like that of Kolbenschlag's, implies that the political leanings of the divine will are revolutionary and anti-Western. In a blistering speech at the first Women in Church conference in Washington DC in 1986, Kolbenschlag excoriated the papacy, the Church, Western civilization, the Judeo-Christian Tradition, the Holy Trinity and monotheism. Then she asked the audience in the name of "our elder brother Jesus" to "be a scandal to patriarchy". She said women must cultivate new 'virtues':

> First, passion – not passion for life but rage and anger against the evils of patriarchy.

Speakers at Women-Church Convergence in Cincinatti in 1987 (theme: "Claiming our Power") included Marjorie Reilly Maguire, board member of the National Abortion Rights Action League, Eleanor Smeal of the pro-abortion National Organisation for Women, and lesbian Charlotte Bunche who accused the Pope and "the right wing" of organizing against lesbian and gay rights. Others described Women-Church as a fluid movement, and as Steichen observes:

> . . . in its fluidity Women-Church uses words to create whatever effect may be desired at any moment.

Rosemary Radford Ruether urged women to give money to her Chicago Catholic Women fund – called 'Mary's Pence' – instead of to the Church. Elizabeth Schussler Fiorenze said that:

Women-Church is a reform movement within the Church, members have not left and will not leave the Church.

She added:

. . . doctrinal fences are really a sign of patriarchy.

At the meeting God was replaced by "Mother-Wisdom" and Jesus was forgotten.

Many well-known names in the Catholic feminist movement attended an American Grail conference in 1982. They included Rosemary Radford Ruether, Elizabeth Schussler Fiorenze, Mary Hunt, Sr Carol Coston, OP and Starhawk. Steichen describes a curious speech entitled "Why Women Need the War God". Religious sociologist Karen McCarthy Brown explained her marriage, in an ecstatic ritual of trance and possession, to the Yoruba voodoo god Oguo.

As she said, with unarguable accuracy:

It can be dangerous to attribute only goodness and light to the realm of the spirit.

Steichen also shows the connections between the New Age Movement and religious feminism which uses the jargon of "cosmic unity, eastern mysticism and eco-feminism". A major chapter documents the thought and writings of Mathew Fox. In 1987 he was the chief celebrant at a bizarre 'Mass of Thanksgiving for the Body' at Holy Name College. Observer Jerald Cooper describes both the litany in praise of the body parts (*te laudamus Domine* for lungs, heart, mitral valve, stomach, colon etc.) and the Wiccan chants and dances as "beyond parody". Steichen reports that according to Fox the Church should focus on the 'original blessing' of creation rather than the "individualistic, sexist, anti-mystical Fall-Redemption theories invented by St Augustine . . ."

Fr Fox's unwillingness to answer directly on abortion is most tendentious. In answer to Steichen's queries he responded:

It's not just mothers who have abortions; its hierarchy who

121

abort things. We have to raise our whole level of awareness about reverence for everything, including ideas and thinkers and movements and artists.

A one year sabbatical was imposed on Fox in December 1988 by the head of his Dominican Order at the insistence of the Vatican. But by January 1990 he was again conducting public seminars in New Zealand and Australia. In December 1989 he visited Auckland where the Catholic Archdiocesan office gave details of his seminars. When asked if he was bringing his witch, Starhawk, with him the reply was "Not on this occasion". There was no indignant repudiation of this suggestion, which was an extraordinary response from an Archdiocesan office.

In chapters headed "The Domino Effect" and "Marching through the Institutions", Steichen illustrates the connections between religious feminism, marxism and liberation theology:

> The reason for Catholic feminism's otherwise puzzling zeal for abortion is its inherently gnostic intent, arising from liberation theology, to build a "new man", isolated from the mediating institution of the family . . . since as the Red Guard of the Catholic cultural revolution, feminists expect to be in control in the new order, they seek what would benefit childless elitists in a collectivist Utopia . . .

Steichen lists the Orders infiltrated with feminism. With many convents in terminal decline, feminist nuns have found jobs in Catholic bureaucracy, and from these vantage points are able to dominate, in such areas as Bishops' pastorals, education strategies and parish policies. While her book focuses on America, it is of great importance to the whole Church because many of its proponents travel and lecture widely, often under the auspices of local Catholic agencies.

In the Catholic Archdiocese of Perth, Sr Sonia Wagner, Director of Pastoral Planning, in her book *Into the Vineyard* writes:

The refusal to admit women to ordination is just one of the symptoms of the disorder that exists in our Church . . . Some women in the Church believe that when the Church is freed from the limited world view of patriarchy, the ordination question will be taken care of itself. There will be a new church and a new sense of ministry for all of us.

Steichen's book concludes on a note of hope – feminists may have made great inroads into religious orders, but those orders which have remained orthodox have formed associations under the banners of the Institute on Religious Life and *Consortium Perfectae Caritatis*. Although most are new and small, some are thriving, including Mother Teresa's Missionaries of Charity, and may continue to grow. Even within the decadent orders, many nuns remain faithful, enduring personal Calvaries.

Furthermore, Catholic laywomen have not been as susceptible to feminism, with their feet firmly planted in the realities of family life and caring for children. They have little inclination for the esoterica of witchcraft or Goddess worship – and the opposition to feminism, both in its religious and secular manifestations, has come from Catholic laywomen all over the world.

James Likoudis, President of Catholics United for the Faith, in Australia, considers feminism to be the greatest single internal threat to the cohesion of of the Catholic Church. *Ungodly Rage* could be a useful resource for our Bishops, if only they would cease to be intimidated by the feminist red guard.

Editor's Note: This article is an edited version of one which appeared in 1991 in the Australian magazine *AD 2000*.

Nine:

Thanks for the Feminine

John Saward

Ingratitude is an ugly thing, a 'monster', says King Lear, a 'marble-hearted fiend', cold contempt for kindness. But gratitude is warm and beautiful, the very seal of friendship, the virtue which makes receiving an act of giving, debt a kind of payment. Pope John Paul's encyclical *Mulieris Dignitatem*, concludes with these exultant words:

> . . . the Church desires to give thanks to the Most Holy Trinity for the mystery of woman and for every woman . . . After all, was it not in and through her that the greatest event in human history – the Incarnation of God Himself – was accomplished? (n 31)

The Holy Father's invitation to offer God 'thanks for the feminine' echoes Our Lord's words to the Samaritan women: "If only you knew the gift of God"! (John 4:10). There is need for a deeper treasuring of God's infinitely precious gifts – the sexual order of His creation and the sacramental order of His Church, marriage and the family, motherhood and virginity, femininity in all its natural richness and supernatural grandeur. Such wholehearted gratitude is urgently needed. The world's salvation depends upon it. For we live at a time when the grace of being a woman has never been more ungratefully spurned, not just by the unthinking sons of Adam, but also by the foolish daughters of Eve. Modern feminism, in its secular but especially its allegedly 'Christian' form, has turned its back on the true genius of womanhood to pursue a programme of male-imitation. By demanding to be and to do all that men are and do, the feminists cravenly proclaim that the male is the sole measure of the human. After all, as is well known, imitation is the sincerest form of flattery. Chesterton realized this long ago when he defined a feminist as "one who dislikes the chief feminine characteristics". *(What's wrong with the World, p 178)*.

Our gratitude should be focused in a special way on one woman, on *the* Woman, God's Virgin Mother, in whom all womanhood is raised up to a nobility beyond compare. Our Lady is the Mother of the Church, sheltering God's people, men, women, and children, under the loving mantle of her prayers. As the Fathers of the Second Vatican Council reminded us, Virgin is the figure, the very personification, of the Church in her final beauty. Those who dissent from the Magisterium tend to look upon the Church as an oppressive, impersonal organization, an It, something to be protested against. Yet the Church embodied in Mary is a She, a Woman, a Mother, someone to be protected by. Those who gratefully and gladly say Yes to the Church's teaching do so because they know that, amidst the shifting sands of the world's fads and fancies, it offers solid, Christ-provided rock, the only sure foundation of our lives.

In the light of Mary, then, we thank God for the feminine. Yes, "in the light of Mary". It is the conviction of the Holy Father and Cardinal Ratzinger that Our Blessed Lady is the God-given remedy for the troubles of our times, in particular, the feminist onslaught on the Church and her faith (cf *The Ratzinger Report*, pp 104f). Just consider what we believe about her. She is Theotokos, the Mother of God, a dignity which places her above all other creatures. "By the power of the Holy Spirit she conceived in her virginal womb and brought into the world Jesus Christ, the Son of God who is of one being with the Father" (Pope John Paul II, *Redemptoris Mater*, n 4). St Paul, in his letter to the Galatians, when he speaks of the Incarnation, refers to God's Son being "born of woman" (4:4; cf MD 3). The word 'woman' is significant. The Blessed Virgin, for the apostles, as for Jesus Himself at Cana and from the Cross, is *the* Woman of human history, the New Eve, the woman whose coming was prophesied in the book of Genesis (cf 3:15). This woman, this Virgin of Israel, stands at the very centre of revelation, for the divine Word becomes man in her flesh and through her faith. She, therefore, "attains a union with God that exceeds all the expections of the human spirit".(MD 3) The highest elevation of human nature took place in the masculine gender, when the divine person of the Son of God became man and male. But the highest elevation of the human person took place in the feminine gender, in Mary, the Virgin Mother of God. In the words of the Byzantine liturgy, she is "more exalted than the cherubim, incomparably more glorious than the seraphim". The greatest after God is a woman. The only truly fulfilled human person, the person already glorified in body as well as soul, is not a male but a female – the Lord's lowly handmaid, the shining Queen of Heaven.

It is as a woman, as Virgin and Mother, that Mary represents the whole human race, indeed all creation, when she says Yes to the Incarnation of God's Son in her womb (cf MD 4). At that great moment it is not male initiative and activism which God asks of humankind but womanly receptivity and openness. Since grace fulfils, does not destroy nature, we can say, we must say, that the fulness of grace given to the Theotokos is the perfection of femininity (cf MD 5), "the new beginning", says Pope John Paul, "of the dignity and vocation of women".(MD 11) The wonderful and unique coincidence in her of virginity and motherhood, far from making her remote from other women, makes her accessible as a model to women in every state of life. Mary, Virgin and Mother, discloses to us that attitude of receptivity which is quintessentially feminine but also the proper disposition of every creature, whether woman or man, with regard to God (cf MD 25). In the light of the Mother of God we see all womanhood anew.

Orthodox Catholic doctrine about and devotion to Our Lady "has not oppressed women but rather has allowed them to appear in their highest dignity".(M Hauke, *Women and the Priesthood?*, p 314). A simple English carol from the last years of the Catholic Middle Ages expresses this beautifully. It is one of several which present the excellence of Our Lady as a reason for respect and honour towards all women. "Wymmen beth bothe goude and truwe/wytnesse on Marie". This song does not emanate from the romantic world of courtly love, but from the heart of a down-to-earth Englishman. Something similar can be seen in the old medieval legend, much loved by Chesterton, that Robin Hood, out of piety towards the Mother of God, would never raid any company which included a woman. I am not claiming that the men and women of the Middle Ages always lived up to this noble vision, but I do believe that there was a deep and general sense in that period that in the uniquely graced womanhood of Our Lady all womanhood is raised up to a dignity beyond compare.

In his study of *The Reformation and the English People*, Professor Jack Scarisbrick contrasts medieval sensitivity to woman with the disdain shown her since the Reformation:

> There were many female saints; heroines of the early Church who had defied husbands and emperors, immensely energetic Anglo-Saxon women who had built nunneries and travelled widely, holy wives and widows . . . as well as holy nuns . . . Above all, there was Mary herself. The numerous dedications and devotions to her, as well as her shrines, show how prominent a place she had in English religious life. All this tempered male authority and . . . asserted the dignity of womanhood. But now (with the Reformation) all that was gone . . . (p 171)

I suspect that the reason why the Protestant denominations

127

have been so vulnerable to the taunts of feminism is that their religion refuses to acknowledge the unique role of woman, of *the* Woman, of Our Lady, in the drama of redemption. In England the Reformation was from the beginning a blow against the dignity of woman. First, Henry VIII discards his lawful wedded wife for another woman, whom later he has killed. Then he dissolves the nunneries and monasteries, including the abbey and shrine at Walsingham, and consigns Our Lady's lovely image to the flames. These combined actions were an attack on the Woman and every woman, on the Mother and every mother, the first blow in a war against, chastity, marriage and the family, which still rages around us. By contrast, the office of Peter, then as now, in its teaching, proclaims and defends woman's true dignity.

As Cardinal Newman saw in the last century, Protestantism's Christology without Mary developed into a Christianity without Christ. The Reformed denominations began by throwing off devotion to the Mother, and now they have ended by abandoning belief in the Son, denying His divinity, virginal conception, and bodily resurrection. What is more, their Maryless doctrine of Christ bequeathed them an impersonal or merely masculine picture of the Church. They see the Church as a clique of interfering clerics rather than a dear loving Mother. (Consider that typical English Protestant phrase 'entering the Church' as a synonym of ordination: it makes the Church seem like a clerical club.) By dishonouring the Virgin Mother, the denominations have devalued both virginity and motherhood. In the sixteenth century, they permitted priests to break their vows and marry; in the twentieth, they allow everyone, even ministers, to divorce and remarry.

There is a lesson to be learnt from the sad history of Protestantism, and it is this: only through 'glad assent' to the teaching of Christ's true Church in all its harmonious wholeness will women, will men, find the road to dignity and fulfilment. The tragic consequences of the Reformation's rejection of devotion to Our Lady confirm the validity of the statement in *Lumen Gentium* that "Mary . . . unites in her person and re-echoes the most important doctrines of the faith" (n 65). She protects the full truth of the Gospel – the truth about Christ and his Church, the truth about man and woman, the truth about marriage, the family, virginity, and every form of life under vow. In the words of an old acclamation, Our Lady "has conquered all heresies".

With Our Lady, in the light of Our Lady, we give thanks to God our Father for the gift of creation, for making women to be women and men to be men. Feminists often quote as an example of the so-called patriarchal mentality the prayer in which the rabbis taught men to bless God for making them men and not women. What feminists forget to tell us is that there is another rabbinic prayer in which women are encouraged to thank God for making them women. The prayer expresses the belief common to both Judaism and Christianity that the sexual differentiation of mankind is willed by God. That is the clear teaching of both creation narratives in Genesis. God did not create, as the Gnostic heretics believed, an androgynous Adam; no, "male and female He created them" (Gen 1:27). Man and woman are equally human; both are created in the image of God, endowed with reason and free will. And yet their equality does not mean uniformity; it is a unity in diversity, a communion in complementarity. "'Masculinity' and 'femininity' are distinct, yet at the same time they complete and explain each other" (MD 25).

Pope John Paul II has given the Church an invaluable resource for understanding and appreciating God's gift of sexual differentiation. I am referring to his theology of the body, which was prepared for in his earlier career as a philosopher, was expounded in a remarkable series of General Audience addresses during the early 1980s, and underlies much of the teaching of *Familiaris Consortio* and *Mulieris Dignitatem*. The Holy Father's starting-point is the truth that human beings are neither angels nor brute beasts but creatures of flesh and spirit in a wonderful unity. Unlike Platonism and all the other dualistic philosophies and religions, Catholic Christianity does not identify the self with the soul. The person is the possessor of the complete nature, body as well as soul. The spiritual, rational, and immortal soul of man is the form of the body, its inward shaping principle. Another way of making the same point is to say that the body is the manifestation of the soul, its expressive incarnation. This means that when God calls man to love, He calls him to express his love in the totality of his nature. As the Holy Father says in *Familiaris Consortio*:

> As an incarnate spirit, that is, a soul which expresses itself in a body and a body informed by an immortal spirit, man is called to love in his unified totality. Love includes the human, body and the body is made a sharer in spiritual love (n 11).

Now the body is either male or female, each ordered by the Creator to the other. The human body has a meaning placed in it by its Maker, says the Pope, and that meaning is nuptual. The body speaks a language, and that language is marriage, the uniting of man and woman to be 'one flesh'. Man is man and not woman; woman is woman and not man; and yet man is made for woman, woman for man. God calls man and woman to find their meaning in an indissoluble union, in a self-giving love that is life-long, faithful, and procreative, in a communion of persons that in some way mirrors the Trinitarian communion of love in God (cf MD 7).

I am underlining this part of the Holy Father's teaching because it provides a bulwark against all those forces in our culture working against the sexual order implanted in nature by God. Once sex is divorced from procreation, it becomes a mere function to be used at will, outside as well as inside marriage, even between men and men or between women and women. It is an extraordinary contradiction, and yet so

130

typical of our times, that people who claim to be 'green', who advocate the natural in all things – natural methods of energy, natural foods and so on, – should tolerate or even promote the unnatural in human behaviour. It is breathtakingly absurd that those who campaign for an unpolluted and fertile earth should recommend the chemical or mechanical sterilizing of woman and man. Against all these follies, Cardinal Ratzinger has reasserted the Church's wisdom:

> For the Church the language of nature (in our case, two sexes complementary to each other yet quite distinct) is also the language of morality (man and woman called to equally noble destinies, both eternal, but different). It is precisely in the name of nature – it is known that Protestant tradition and, in its wake, that of enlightenment mistrust this concept – that the Church raises her voice against the temptation to project persons and their destiny according to mere human plans, to strip them of their individuality and, in consequence, of dignity. To respect biology is to respect God Himself, hence to safeguard His creatures (*The Ratzinger Report*, p 97f).

"A woman cannot receive the Sacrament of Order, and therefore cannot fulfil the proper function of the ministerial priesthood" (*Christifideles Laici* 51). In the light of Our Lady it is clear that the necessary maleness of the ministerial priesthood does not in any sense imply the inferiority of the Christian laywoman. The impossibility of women's ordination stems not from an outmoded misogyny, but from the unique and unrepeatable grandeur of women in the creative and saving purposes of God. It is to the glory of woman that she cannot be ordained.

As Pope John Paul has shown so beautifully in *Mulieris Dignitatem*, Our Blessed Lord, even in the eyes of His contemporaries, was regarded as "a promoter of woman's true dignity" (MD 12). His disciples were amazed that He was prepared to talk, heart to heart, to the Samaritan woman (cf John 4:7). He ignored the legal impurity of the woman who suffered from a flow of blood (cf Matt 9:20–22). By pardoning the woman taken in adultery, He showed that a woman's sin must not be shown greater severity than a man's (cf John 8:11). Women showed a special sensitivity to Our Lord's mission: St Luke tells that St Mary Magdalene and several other women accompanied Him and His apostles on His preaching journey (cf Luke 8:2f). It is women who are at the forefront by His cross, while all the disciples, save one, desert Him. It is the women who are the first to go to the tomb, the first to find it empty, the first to embrace the pierced feet of the Risen One, the first to announce the truth to the apostles. And yet Our Lord does not call women to be His apostles. And He does so, not because He was conforming to the prejudices of His day, but because a male priesthood was exactly what He wanted. He acted in sovereign freedom. He wanted woman's splendour to shine through in another, in an even greater, way.

To understand this more deeply, we must consider Our Lord's Sacrifice on the Cross and its sacramental representation in the Mass. Jesus is Priest and Victim as Bridegroom: the love with which He "gives" His Body and "pours out" His Blood is spousal, a husbandly love. He became human and male and died on the Cross in order to marry the whole human race in that bond of indissoluble love which we call the New Covenant. "As the Redeemer of the world, Christ is the Bridegroom of the Church" (MD 26). Now the Eucharist is the Sacrament of our Redemption, and so it is also the "Sacrament of the Bridegroom and the Bride" (*Ibid.*). It expresses the "redemptive act of Christ the Bridegroom towards the Church the Bride". The celebrant of Holy Mass has to be male because he acts "in the person of Christ". He plays the part of the self-sacrificing Bridegroom in the sacred drama. He is Christ's 'image' or 'sacramental sign'. He must, therefore, be male.

Woman, in the plan of God, was destined for something incomparably greater even than ministerial priesthood. Only a man can be a priest, but only a woman can be and is Mother of God. It is a woman, not a man, who represents the whole human race in saying Yes to the Incarnation. It is a woman, not a man, that is the Church's supreme model and embodiment as Christ's Bride and our Mother. It is femininity, rather than masculinity, which symbolizes the proper attitude of the soul before God (cf MD 25). There is a kind of poverty about the male which Christ puts to use in ordination. The man's role in generation is outside himself, in the womb of the woman, and in utter dependence on the power of God. Woman, by contrast, receives and then retains and nourishes the gift of life within herself. Similarly, men image Christ in the priesthood, but they are not Christ. Their inadequacy is shown up by the greatness of the part they play. By contrast, women symbolize creation and at the same time they are creatures. In other words, women embody the very values they symbolize. Men do no more than point.

Developing an idea taken from theology of Hans Urs von Balthasar, the Holy Father reminds us, in *Mulieris Dignitatem*, that the Church as a whole is Marian, feminine, open to receive the life and truth of her Head, while the male hierarchy, the Petrine/apostolic ministry, is just one part of the Church, with the humble vocation to serve the feminine whole.

Mary Immaculate precedes all others, including obviously Peter himself and the apostles. This is so, not only because Peter and the apostles, being born of the human race under the burden of sin, form part of the Church which is "holy from out of sinners", but also because their triple function has no other purpose except to form the Church in line with the ideal of sanctity already programmed and prefigured in Mary. A contemporary theologian has rightly stated that Mary is "Queen of the apostles without any pretensions to apostolic powers: she has other and greater powers" (MD 27, footnote 55, citing von Balthasar).

As wife and mother, woman has been entrusted with the human being in a special way. The first person a man ever knows, the first protective presence, the first love, the first smile, is that of a woman, his mother. His first home is her body (cf MD 19). As Chesterton once said, every human being comes into existence quite literally 'enveloped' in femininity. This "special communion with the mystery of life" (cf MD 18) which is prepared for in the physiological and psychological constitution of women, give them a "specific sensitivity towards the human person and all that constitutes the individual's true welfare, beginning with the fundamental value of life" (CL 51). In virtue of their God-given nature, women, our wives and mothers and sisters, have a capacity to bring us down to earth, to lead us back to realities, the personal realities, of life. It is with these uniquely feminine gifts (which the virgin or celibate woman enjoys in a specially deep way) that the Christian woman fulfils her mission in the Church.

We all know that only men can be ordained to the priesthood, but we forget that only women can be consecrated as virgins. The reason for this is that, according to the teaching of the Fathers and the rite restored by Pope Paul VI in 1970, the consecrated woman virgin represents and anticipates the Church as eschatological Bride of Christ, the Bride that St John saw descending from Heaven, "adorned for her husband" (Apoc 21:2). Thus, whether in consecrated virginity or in the Sacrament of Matrimony, every Christian woman is called to be married, is called to self-giving bridal love.

A woman is 'married' either through the sacrament of marriage or spiritually through marriage to Christ. In both cases marriage signifies the 'sincere gift of the person' of the bride to the groom (MD 21).

Because miraculously, by the power of God, virginity and motherhood coincide in one woman, they are mutually illuminating for every woman. Consecrated virginity makes possible an extraordinarily fruitful motherhood 'in the Spirit', which can be seen in the lives of women religious throughout the Church's history. The all-embracing love of a Mother Teresa is the most striking modern example. And for the married woman, there is the spiritual dimension of her physical motherhood. As the Holy Father says in *Mulieris Dignitatem*, "the motherhood of every woman . . . is . . . not only 'of flesh and blood': it expresses a profound 'listening to the Word of the living God' and readiness to 'safeguard' this Word" (MD 19). In other words, the natural motherly qualities of receptivity and protectiveness are the foundation of that special sensitivity to the religious which seems to characterize women.

Our Lady is the model of our gratitude, as she is of everything else that is Christian. Full of grace, she is full of gratefulness. The Immaculate better than anyone knows the gift of God, the treasure He has consigned to woman's safe-keeping. When her cousin extols her, Mary magnifies God, praises Him for the gift of His Son in her womb. As Bishop Fulton Sheen once said, in shortened form the Magnificat says simply this: "Thank God". That is all I have been trying to say. Thank God for creation, thank God for redemption, thank God for Our Lady, thank God for the Pope, thanks for the feminine.

FEMINISM v. MANKIND
edited by Christine M Kelly

Foreword by Baroness Elles

Contributors:

Alice von Hildebrand (USA)	Katarina Runske (Sweden)
Babette Francis (Australia)	Joanna Bogel (UK)
Cornelia Ferreira (Canada)	Patricia Morgan (UK)
Betty Steele (Canada)	Valerie Riches (UK)
Mary Kenny (Ireland)	Robert Whelan (UK)

A book which challenges the myths and excesses propounded by the radical feminists. The authors express their anger and concern at the extent to which extreme feminist aims have already been carried out in different parts of the world, and the damage done in every field of activity.

A theme taken up by several contributors is the constant and widespread denigration of women who want to stay at home to look after their children, which many women find offensive. In Canada they have been referred to as "house slugs". Katarina Runske from Sweden quotes Nobel prize winner Mrs Alvar Myrdal: **"It is still possible for weak, stupid, lazy, unambitious and otherwise lesser equipped individuals to remain and make their way within domestic work, both as housewives and servants. As for the rest, prostitution is always available".**

The extent to which some feminists go to try to make women into carbon-copy men is well documented. Swedish girls who choose the traditionally male professions receive extra points when they enter college as part of a special quota system. In parts of Australia, under the Jobs for Local Roads scheme half of those employed in road building must be female. In Canada, laws and quota systems have resulted in great injustices against men.

Cornelia Ferreira in Canada reminds us that those planning to conquer the world consider the corruption of women as indispensable to their schemes: **" . . . we can reform the world if we reform women".**

In her foreword, Baroness Elles says:

"This work will make a valuable contribution to the debunking of creeping popularist theories which have held the forefront of the debate for far too long. It rightly seeks to restore the balance of common sense, based on practical experience, professional knowledge and innate wisdom. It should be welcomed by a wide range of readers who, whatever their background or specific interests, are concerned with the peaceful and just development of our society."

The book ends with a note of encouragement and optimism. Betty Steele tells how the girls in a Miss Teen Canada competition made headlines when they did battle with the radical feminists and were not prepared to go along with them. The contestants responded:

"We girls want to be considered 'persons', not segregated into a corner of the ring as 'Women's Libbers' who come out punching and clawing against men at every imagined inequality . . . men are not our enemies. We love our fathers, our brothers, our boy-friends and we still believe in ordinary happy marriages in spite of those divorce statistics . . . which we blame on the Women's Liberation Movement."

FEMINISM v. MANKIND
Edited by Christine M Kelly

96 pages   size 210 x 145mm   Price: £4.95 plus 40p p&p

Published by **FAMILY PUBLICATIONS : WICKEN : MILTON KEYNES : MK19 6BU**

Telephone: 0908 57234   Fax: 0908 57331